PENGUIN BOOKS

STEP BY STEP: THE BIOGRAPHY OF PEMBA GELJE SHERPA

Mark Powell is a British-born author and screenplay writer who has immersed himself in Singapore's vibrant culture for the past twenty-five years and weaves his experiences into his literary works, captivating readers with his unique perspective. Powell's writing style is explosive, leaving readers on the edge of their seats with electrifying narratives that delve deep into the human psyche and explore the complexities of relationships and personal growth. Powell has also lived in New York City, Los Angeles and London.

What sets Powell apart is his ability to tell stories in a brutally realistic manner, allowing readers to connect with his characters at a profound level. These characters —strong, clever, and fearless—navigate life's challenges in compelling and thought-provoking ways.

While Powell's versatility as a writer is evident, his preferred genre is crime thrillers. Within this genre, he expertly crafts suspenseful plots, skilfully intertwining elements of mystery and intrigue. However, Powell's talent extends beyond crime thrillers, as he has also written in other genres, such as psychological thrillers, action and adventure, romantic comedies, and biographies.

In addition to his fiction works, Powell occasionally delves into non-fiction, drawing from his thirty-year career in the world's largest financial institutions. Through his non-fiction works, he offers unique insights and perspectives, showcasing his expertise in leadership, project execution, and mentorship.

One of Powell's remarkable talents is his ability to tailor his writing for different audiences, effortlessly transitioning between writing for adults and young adults. This versatility showcases his deep understanding of the nuances of storytelling for different demographics.

With readers' and critics' recognition and praise, Powell's ability to engage and entertain audiences has earned him a loyal following. Whether it be his gripping crime thrillers or enlightening non-fiction works, Powell's books continue to resonate with people from all walks of life.

More specifically, Powell's love of the outdoors, nature and mountain trekking is when he feels most alive.

T0290124

STEP BY STEP

THE BIOGRAPHY OF PEMBA GELJE SHERPA

MARK POWELL

PENGUIN BOOKS

An imprint of Penguin Random House

PENGUIN BOOKS

USA | Canada | UK | Ireland | Australia
New Zealand | India | South Africa | China | Southeast Asia

Penguin Books is part of the Penguin Random House group of companies
whose addresses can be found at global.penguinrandomhouse.com

Published by Penguin Random House SEA Pte Ltd
9, Changi South Street 3, Level 08-01,
Singapore 486361

First published in Penguin Books by Penguin Random House SEA 2023
Copyright © Mark Powell 2023

ISBN 9789815204681

www.penguin.sg

*To every Sherpa and Mountain Guide who sacrificed their lives
to save and protect others, and to those brave souls who rest in
eternal sleep upon the slopes of our great mountains.*

"प्रत्येक शेर्पा र पर्वत गाइडको जीवन पर्वाह गर्दै अन्यहरूलाई उद्धार गर्न र संरक्षण
गर्न बलिदान गरेका छन्, र हाम्रो महान पर्वतहरूको धाराहरूमा आन्तरिक निद्रामा
बसेर।"

To my family:

*Father: Phunurbu Sherpa
Mother: Dawa Pasang Sherpa
Brother: Pemba Ongchu Sherpa
Brother: Pemba Chongba Sherpa
Sister: Lakpa Yangji Sherpa
Brother: Pema Rigzin Sherpa
Brother: Lakpa Sonam Sherpa
Sister: Mingma Chamji Sherpa
Sister: Mingma Yangji Sherpa*

CONTENTS

Acknowledgements   xi

Foreword   xiii

How this book came to be   xvii

A note from Pemba Gelje Sherpa   xxi

Preface   xxv

Foreshadow   xxix

The Sherpa people   xxxiii

1. The Call of the Mountains   1

2. A Student Monk   8

3. A Sherpa's Path   12

4. A Moment of Inner Reflection   19

5. Sherpa Brotherhood   22

6. A Mountain's Lesson   25

7. Big Brother's Footsteps   32

8. Step by Step Upon Everest   36

9. A Lesson in Life   42

10. Conquering Everest   46

11. The Courageous Rescues   53

12. Beyond Everest   59

13. The Language of the Mountains   66

14. A Life of Service   72

15. Recognitions and Accolades   77

16. Earthquake, 2015   83

17. The Mountaineer's Code   89

18. Lessons From the Summits   95

19. The Magic of the Himalayas   100

20. The Legacy Continues   106

21. A Journey of the Senses   111

22. A Life of Balance   116

23. The Mountains as Teachers   121

24. The Mountains Within Us All   126

25. A Love Letter to the Mountains   131

26. The Spirit of Adventure   136
27. The Power of Human Connection   141
28. The Endless Summits   146
29. Frozen In Time   151
30. The Frozen Souls Who Deserve Respect   155
31. To Climb, or Not to Climb   157

A Mountaineer's Prayer   161
Epilogue   163
Gallery of Memories   166
In Memory of the Brave   168
In Memory of My Brave Sherpa Brothers   170
Pemba Gelje Sherpa Notable Summits   173
Notable Rescue Missions   174
Awards and Appreciations   175
Affiliations   176
The Best Tip Ever   177

ACKNOWLEDGEMENTS

Writing a biography is not a solitary endeavour; it's a collective effort that draws strength from the many who support, provide inspiration, and offer contributions. As the author of *'Step by Step,'* I am deeply grateful to the following individuals who have made this book a reality:

Fei Zhao: To my beloved wife, Fei Zhao, whose unwavering belief in Pemba Gelje's story ignited the spark that led to the creation of this book. Your adventurous spirit and insistence that Pemba Gelje's story be told have been my guiding light throughout this journey.

Carla Perez: Thank you, Carla, for lending your eloquence and insight to craft a powerful foreword that sets the tone for Pemba Gelje's extraordinary story. Your words have added depth and resonance to this biography.

Cover Designers and Editors: A heartfelt thank you to the creative minds and meticulous editors who shaped this book. Your dedication to excellence has transformed mere words into a captivating narrative.

Pemba Gelje's Family and Friends: Pemba Gelje's story is a testament to the profound impact of family and friendship. Your support, stories, and memories have enriched this book and made it a tribute to the tight-knit bonds of community and kinship.

The Village of Kharikhola: To the warm-hearted community of Kharikhola, where Pemba Gelje's journey began, thank you for welcoming us with open arms and sharing your traditions, wisdom, and hospitality. You are an integral part of this narrative.

Climbing Sherpas and Mountain Guides: Every climbing Sherpa and mountain guide, past and present, who has shared the arduous paths and soaring summits with Pemba has left an indelible mark on this story. Your camaraderie and expertise inspire us all.

The IFMGA: The International Federation of Mountain Guides Associations, for your dedication to safety, professionalism, and the preservation of mountain environments. Your work ensures that climbers like Pemba can pursue their passions safely.

Fellow Climbers: To every soul who has ascended alongside Pemba on the challenging slopes of mountains, thank you for being part of his incredible journey. Your stories and companionship have contributed to the rich tapestry of his life.

Mountain Gods and Spirits: We acknowledge the sacred presence of the mountain gods and spirits, who watch over climbers and bless them with safe passage. May their eternal grace guide and protect those seeking the heights.

In the grand tapestry of Pemba Gelje Sherpa's life, you have woven a thread of inspiration, encouragement, and support. This book is a tribute to the collective effort that has brought his remarkable journey to light. With heartfelt gratitude, we thank you for participating in this incredible adventure.

Sincerely,

Mark Powell

Author & Mountain Explorer

FOREWORD

When I first saw Pemba Gelje in 2014, he emerged from a beam of sunlight as if he had been beamed down upon the earth from a space-craft. Of course, he hadn't. He wore a light blue down jacket, slate grey trekking pants and what I later observed as his trademark, a rather grubby-looking cotton snood rolled down around his neck. An oblig-atory pair of sunglasses were perched upon his head. His sun-kissed young face carried the warmest smiles, putting me at ease. He was guiding at the time two very experienced Italian climbers named Antonio and Giorgio.

I had just arrived at basecamp and was about to embark upon an expedi-tion to ascend, and as one always hopes to safely descend, Cho Oyu, the 'Turquoise Goddess' and the sixth highest mountain in the world, towering up at 8,188 meters above sea level. Before that trip, I had not had the opportunity to meet or interact with a Sherpa, and my percep-tion was like that of many: that they are extraordinarily and incredibly, almost superhuman strong, and their empathy and warm-hearted nature make them always willing to be at the service of others. I had also observed and learned during my time as a mountaineer that they were known to risk and sacrifice their own lives to save others, often strangers. They, indeed, are the guardians of the Himalayan mountains.

On this occasion, I embarked on my expedition to Cho Oyu without companions or high-attitude porters. Although plenty of people were around, I could have invited or paid to join me. But I decided to climb alone. I was looking to find my inner fire. I had something to prove to myself, having attempted to climb Everest the year before, in 2013, without oxygen. My climb had to be aborted at around 8650 feet due to the cold and wind on that day at altitude.

So, here I was a year later, meeting Pemba Gelje for the first time. But I was carrying a heavy pack and the mental burden of scars from that day in 2013. They were the scars of not only failing to reach the summit of Everest but also from social pressure. The bullying and criticism I received after that expedition was so intense it caused me to enter a depressive state of mind. I was also deeply angry with myself and had lost all confidence in my abilities. But Cho Oyu had reached out into my psyche and presented an opportunity to heal.

Initially, my relationship with Pemba Gelje felt like one of kindness, given I had decided to join his party of climbers, and they had accepted me. As the days passed, Pemba Gelje and I began to engage in more profound and extended conversations centred around the philosophy of life, climbing and the majestical beauty and spirit of the mountains. Pemba Gelje's zest and respect for life and all things living upon it was contagious. Still, he also had this inner peace that could be seen in his eyes and his years as a young monk in a monastery taught him the wisdom of birth, life, death, and how to honour his parents, family and ancestors.

Cho Oyu had become, without me realising it, a temple, and Pemba Gelje was my spiritual guide. And so it was that not only did the mountain call my name and bless me with an incredible mountain guide, but my friendship with Pemba Gelje was a gateway to the new me, and he became a guide in that process.

Before and during the expedition on Cho Oyu, there were many issues to heal with my soul and mind and little by little; I started to open up and listen, to understand and learn. Pemba Gelje taught me that I had succeeded in 2013 on Everest; I had grown, given I had already arrived there and taken the first step. Every step after that was another success until the elements of nature decided I had achieved enough. I had not failed at all. Instead, I had succeeded in coming back alive and gaining vital experience. I finally summited Cho Oyu in October 2014, with Pemba Gelje by my side.

To get a true sense of who Pemba Gelje is- he is not about being the fastest man to summit a peak, nor is he interested in how many mountains a mortal human can climb within a set number of days or months. He certainly does not lose sleep over how many social media followers he gains or losses in a single day.

Pemba Gelje is about respecting the mountains, their spirit, their power, the danger, their very existence, and the Sherpa culture that has been born out of them and merged with them.

Love from Carla Perez – Mountaineer & Mountain Guide, 2022

Carla Perez is the First Latin woman to summit K2,
Everest, Makalu and Cho Oyu without the aid of Oxygen

HOW THIS BOOK CAME TO BE

In the shadow of the Himalayas, where adventure meets the extraordinary, lies the captivating story of Pemba Gelje Sherpa. This biography unravels the life of a man whose path to greatness was paved with challenges, humour, and resilience. But before we delve into Pemba Gelje's fascinating life, let's rewind to the peculiar circumstances that led to the creation of this enthralling story.

It all began when Fei Zhao, an intrepid explorer with a penchant for conquering towering peaks, returned home from her daring expedition to Mera Peak in Nepal. Pemba Gelje Sherpa had been her guiding light through the treacherous terrain of the Himalayas, and what an impression he left! They had become snowbound at Lukla for a week, and what else to do than drink hot tea, eat Sherpa stew and talk?

They had to wait for the airport to thaw; no flights were coming in, and no flights were going out. Fei was so obsessed with Pemba Gelje's charisma and incredible stories of his mountain adventures that she insisted her spouse, that's me, the one and only, must meet this extraordinary guide and share his story with the world.

Picture this: Fei, breathless from her Himalayan adventure, bursts through the front door, her enthusiasm matching the altitude she had just descended from. She regaled me with stories of Pemba Gelje's unorthodox jokes at the most perilous moments, his uncanny ability to summon a hot cup of tea out of thin air, and how he seemed to carry the Himalayan peaks in his back pocket. As she spoke, her eyes sparkled with the enthusiasm only the mountains can ignite.

Fei Zhao - 2021

And so, here you are, about to embark on a literary journey to unearth the incredible life of Pemba Gelje Sherpa. From his humble beginnings in the remote Sherpa villages of Nepal to scaling some of the world's highest summits, Pemba Gelje's story is a testament to the indomitable human spirit. Prepare to be awed, amused, and inspired as we unveil the man behind the legend, all thanks to Fei Zhao's irresistible insistence and a newfound appreciation for Pemba Gelje's humour in the most unlikely places.

Join us as we traverse the breathtaking landscapes of the Himalayas and unravel the many layers of Pemba Gelje's life. '*Step by Step*' is not just a biography; it's a journey through the heart and soul of a man who defied gravity, both physically and metaphorically, and it all started with a wife who believed in the power of a good adventure and an even better storyteller.

A NOTE FROM PEMBA GELJE SHERPA

This biography, written by a dear friend, does not follow the conventional narrative of glittering Hollywood stars, former political titans, Netflix, or social media sensations boasting millions of followers. It refrains from the notion of exceptionalism. Instead, it delves into a collection of genuine, unadorned stories from the annals of my life, presented with unwavering authenticity and devoid of embellishment.

Nostalgia and sentimentality hold no allure for me, nor do I harbour any early retirement aspirations, a theme that often pervades memoirs. In my perspective, life is an ongoing journey, each day serving as a new beginning, for none of us can truly predict the duration of our earthly sojourn. This book does not serve as a technical manual, imparting climbing advice or proffering lectures on the intricacies of the craft. However, within its pages are some lessons to be learned from my experiences, aiming to assist and share the wisdom accrued through my expeditions.

This biography is not a platform to dictate my actions or trumpet my achievements to inflate my ego. Instead, it is a genuine testament to my open, honest, and unpretentious life. It is a repository of stories, insights, and philosophies meant for your objective consideration, understanding, and, if you so choose, subjective adoption. By assimilating these stories, you may discover the power to alter or perceive your reality through a different lens.

Throughout my life, adventures have been both consequential and enlightening. They have traversed the spectrum from educational to humorous, harrowing to whimsical, often not by design but by their essence. An innate optimism guides my perspective, while humility has served as a profound equaliser, levelling the terrain of my existence. This virtue has enabled me to confront pain, loss, and the erosion of trust, fostering personal growth and averting the pitfalls of arrogance. I make no claims to perfection; I acknowledge my fallibility and accept the metaphorical 'Yak shit' I occasionally step in. We all encounter these challenges—roadblocks, mistakes, deceptions, illnesses, and the disheartening chasm between our desires and life's offerings. It is the human condition. The art lies in deeming such encounters as fortuitous or devising strategies to minimise their recurrence.

As you embark on this narrative journey, I expect you to appreciate it for its unreserved honesty and genuine humility. Furthermore, it imparts wisdom as a mirror reflecting the universal human experience and a guide for navigating the labyrinth of life.

A word of caution: If you intend to delve into the story of a Sherpa who transcended poverty to amass untold wealth through endorsements, one who lays claim to being the paramount, the swiftest, or the most astute mountaineer in the Himalayas, you may find yourself disappointed. I am simply Pemba Gelje Sherpa, content with my identity, and I am entirely at peace with that fact.

*Pemba
Gelje*

A note from Pemba Gelje Sherpa

PREFACE

Have you ever wondered what it would be like to walk amongst giants? To traverse the rugged terrain and inhale the crisp mountain air while knowing you are on the same path as those who conquer the highest peaks on Earth? Imagine feeling the ground beneath your feet, bare and connected to the very soul of the Himalayas. This is the world of Pemba Gelje, a man who embodies the spirit of the Sherpa people and whose life is a testament to the power of determination, strength, and unwavering humility.

As I embarked on this journey to write the biography of Pemba Gelje, I wasn't expecting to be captivated by a man whose smile could light up the darkest corners of the world. His presence was like a warm embrace, an invitation to delve deeper into his story, and I couldn't help but be drawn into his world of wild rivers, soaring peaks and deep valleys.

Our first meeting took place in the bustling chaos of Kathmandu airport. Amidst the cacophony of sounds and the hurried footsteps of travellers, he stood, his broad grin reaching out to me with a sparkle in his eyes. Pemba exuded a sense of tranquillity that made me feel instantly at ease as if the world's weight had been lifted off my shoulders. He greeted me with a traditional white blessing scarf, symbolising his kindness and acceptance. 'Nice to meet you, Sir, namaste,' he said with a humble nod. Little did I know that this encounter would signal the beginning of a remarkable journey that forever changed how I saw the world.

In the following days, I walked alongside Pemba on the fabled trails of the Everest Base Camp (EBC), immersing myself in the essence of his existence. Each step brought me closer to understanding the true nature of this man – a Sherpa whose unwavering resilience and unwavering dedication had earned him the title of one of the finest mountain guides in the world. But it wasn't just his expertise on treacherous peaks that astonished me; it was his ability to remain grounded amidst the grandeur of the Himalayas. Pemba Gelje, a man of iron, stood tall as a beacon of humility, reminding all who crossed his path that the mountains were not to be conquered but to be respected.

As I listened to his stories, I marvelled at the incredible tapestry of his life. From his humble beginnings in the high plains of the Khumbu region, where he grew up barefoot, to his triumphs and joys, Pemba Gelje's journey was one of sheer willpower and unyielding determination. He spoke of the sacrifices made by the Sherpa community, a group often overshadowed and misrepresented but whose unwavering spirit and unwavering support were the backbone of countless expeditions to the highest peaks. Pemba Gelje's story was not just a story of personal triumph but a celebration of the Sherpas' resilience and invaluable contributions to mountaineering.

Through his candid reflections, Pemba invites us into a world where fear and courage walk hand in hand. He takes us on a rollercoaster of emotions, from moments of uproarious laughter to spine-chilling accounts that send shivers down our spines. And yet, amidst the triumphs and tribulations, Pemba Gelje's spirit radiates an indomitable warmth that captivates and inspires.

Step by Step is not just a biography; it is an intimate exploration of the human spirit, a testament to the power of perseverance and the unbreakable bonds that tie the Sherpa people to the mountains. Pemba

Gelje's journey must be heard, his story a symphony of hope and courage that resonates with all who dare to dream.

So, join me on this incredible adventure as we tread in the footsteps of giants. Let us immerse ourselves in the sheer majesty of the Himalayas and bask in the radiant light of Pemba Gelje's smile. Step by Step, we will journey through the mountaintops and valleys of Nepal, guided by a man whose strength and humility will forever leave an indelible mark on our souls. Together, we will discover the true power of the human spirit and the profound beauty within each of us.

The majestic Himalayas

FORESHADOW

In the ever-evolving tapestry of the literary realm, particular chronicles stand as resolute sentinels against the relentless passage of time, their narratives delving deep into the recesses of our very souls. These are the sagas that kindle the flames of inspiration, impart wisdom, and stoke the enthusiasm of our spirits. With a profound sense of privilege and the deepest honour, I humbly present to you '*Step by Step* ,' an extraordinary biography that unfurls the life story of Pemba Gelje, a Sherpa whose existence stands as a breathtaking testament to the indomitable spirit of humanity.

As a son of Nepal, Pemba Gelje was nurtured amidst the towering peaks of the Khumbu region, nestled within the enigmatic embrace of the Everest territory in Northeast Nepal. His journey, however, extends beyond the boundaries of mere geographical exploration; it is a profound odyssey into the very essence of the human experience. '*Step by Step*' unveils an unfiltered portrait of Pemba Gelje's remarkable life, painted with brushstrokes of sensitivity, elegance, and a delightful dash of humour, capable of evoking both profound awe and hearty laughter.

From the very opening words of this biography, you shall sense the radiant warmth that radiates from Pemba Gelje's very being, enveloping each page like a comforting blanket. His infectious smile, resonant laughter, and genuine humility shall beckon you into his world—a world where mountains are not mere obstacles to be surmounted but sacred realms that demand our reverence and respect.

In this intro, I invite you to peer into the chapters that await your perusal. Together, we shall embark upon a voyage through the very heart of Pemba Gelje's existence, commencing with his deep-seated affinity for the majestic Himalayas and the magnetic allure that enticed him toward a life intertwined with the art of mountaineering. We shall traverse the awe-inspiring landscapes, fathom the spiritual significance that these colossal peaks hold, and unravel the profound impact they have etched upon Pemba Gelje's life.

We shall tread alongside Pemba on his path as he navigates the perilous terrains of the mountaineering realm, confronting both physical and emotional adversities with unwavering resolve. We shall bear witness to his triumphs and tribulations and delve into the profound influence of his Sherpa heritage upon his arduous journey.

Within the pages of this biography, we shall embark upon a rollercoaster ride, ascending to the euphoric pinnacles of his triumphs—conquering Everest multiple times and K2—only to descend into the depths of heart-wrenching losses, both witnessed and endured. This narrative shall offer an enthralling exploration of the peaks and troughs of a life lived on the precipice.

Delving deep into the intricate tapestry of Pemba Gelje's soul, I shall unfurl the complex layers of his persona, unravelling the threads of his passions, joys, and unwavering dedication to his life's calling. In doing so, I shall not merely extol Pemba as a brave hero but provide an intimate glimpse into the heart of a man who personifies the most accurate form of humility.

Ultimately, we shall embark upon a vacation of inspiration as the story of Pemba Gelje's life unfolds. We shall unearth the profound lessons he garnered from his experiences and the boundless power of the human spirit to surmount any obstacle. This volume shall serve as a testament to the indomitable strength of human resolve and the limitless potential inherent within every individual.

As we delve deeper into the pages of '*Step by Step*,' we shall be treated to a symphony of hope, courage, and resilience—a symphony orches-trated by the extraordinary life of Pemba Gelje. His story shall challenge us, elevate us, and etch an indelible mark upon the very core of our beings. With each page turned, we shall be reminded of the majestic grandeur of the Himalayas and the indomitable spirit of the Sherpa people.

Therefore, dear reader, I cordially invite you to join me on this extraordinary odyssey. Let us traverse hand in hand with Pemba Gelje through Nepal's lofty peaks and mystical valleys. Are you prepared? Let us commence step by step.

THE SHERPA PEOPLE

Exploring the Sherpa Culture:

Before embarking on this journey into the life of Pemba Gelje Sherpa, it was imperative to delve into the heart of the Sherpa culture. To truly understand Pemba, one must first understand the cultural tapestry from which he emerges.

For many, the Sherpa culture remains an enigmatic treasure trove, obscured by misconceptions and stereotypes. Too often, it is seen as a hardy group of people, their faces adorned with warm smiles, bearing the burdens of heavy loads up treacherous mountain slopes for the benefit of affluent tourists and mountaineering expeditions. However, the Sherpa identity is far more profound.

Roots of the Sherpa People:

Sherpas trace their origins to Tibetan roots, occupying the high valleys encircling the base of Mount Everest in north-eastern Nepal. The term 'Sherpa' itself finds its roots in the Tibetan language, where 'Shar Pa' translates to 'people who live in the east.' This moniker, over time, has become synonymous with the Sherpa community.

While Sherpa tradition asserts their migration to Nepal from the Kham region of eastern Tibet over a millennium ago, historians suggest a different narrative. They speculate that the Sherpas were once nomadic herders forcibly displaced from their homeland east of Tibet due to conflicts with aggressive neighbours. In search of greener pastures, they embarked on a journey that led them across the formidable Himalayas to their current homeland in north-eastern Nepal.

Sherpas as Mountaineering Maestros:

The Sherpa people are celebrated worldwide as elite mountaineers and Himalayan experts. They played an invaluable role in the early explorations of the region, serving as guides on treacherous peaks and high-altitude passes, especially during Mount Everest expeditions. Regrettably, today, the term 'Sherpa' is often misused by foreigners to refer to any porter, guide, or support staff engaged in Himalayan mountaineering endeavours, regardless of their ethnicity. Consequently, it has metamorphosed into a colloquial expression for any guide or mentor in various contexts.

Some attribute the Sherpas' exceptional mountaineering prowess to genetics cultivated by centuries of high-altitude living. Genetic adaptations include a unique capacity for haemoglobin-binding and the ability to produce nearly double the nitric oxide in the bloodstream.

Unraveling the Sherpa Persona:

But beyond their mountaineering fame, who are the Sherpa people?

The Sherpa language, known as Sherpa or Sherpali, is a Tibetan dialect with influences from neighbouring tongues. It belongs to the Tibeto-Burman branch of the Sino-Tibetan language family. Sherpas primarily employ Tibetan script for their written language, while Nepali is used in interactions with other ethnic groups.

Presently, the Sherpa population is estimated at around 45,000 individuals. They predominantly inhabit the Khumbu and Solu Khumbu regions south of Mount Everest. Sherpa communities extend eastward into Kulung and westward into the Dudh Kosi and Rolwaling Rivers valleys west of Solu-Khumbu. Additionally, they can be found in the Lantang-Helambu region north of Kathmandu, with a significant Sherpa population residing in the capital city itself. Smaller Sherpa communities can even be found in Nepal's Terai region. Further afield, Sherpa settlements dot the Indian state of Sikkim and the hill towns of Darjeeling and Kalimpong.

Sherpas are distinguishable by their relatively fair complexion, short stature, and distinctive facial features reminiscent of their Tibetan lineage. Their settlements are perched on the flanks of the towering hills that reach down into Nepal from the Himalayan crest. Deep gorges and a complex terrain of steep ridges and narrow valleys characterise these regions. Notably, Sherpa villages sit at some of the highest elevations of human habitation, with communities in Khumbu between 10,000 to 14,000 feet (approximately 3,000 to 4,300 meters) above sea level. Here, winters are harsh, blanketing the landscape with snow from November to February. During this period, most able-bodied Sherpas migrated to lower altitudes, leaving only the elderly in the villages. Spring commences in February, and with it, the return of the people for the New Year festival. The subsequent three months are dedicated to preparing fields and sowing crops. Summer temperatures fluctuate with altitude. In Nauje village, situated at 11,287 feet (3,440 meters) in Khumbu, the July mean temperature hovers around 54°F (12°C). The monsoon season, characterised by heavy rains, typically spans May to August. August to November marks another stretch of fair weather, ideal for harvesting crops.

Sherpa Hospitality and Tradition:

Sherpa hospitality is deeply ingrained in their culture. Guests in a Sherpa home must never leave unfed or without a drink. Tibetan tea or beer typically welcomes guests, with those of high status treated to snacks or even full meals. Sherpa homes allow guests unrestricted access to the kitchen and designated worship area.

In Sherpa society, a child's naming ceremony is a momentous occasion. Upon birth, the local lama (Buddhist spiritual leader) is informed of the event and the exact time it transpired. The lama then uses this information to determine the child's name and the timing of the naming ceremony. Often, children are named based on the day of the week they were born. For example, a baby born on a Friday might be called 'Pasang,' the Sherpa word for 'Friday.' The lama, relatives, and neighbours convene to celebrate this significant event with a feast.

Sherpa children grow under the guidance of their mothers, as fathers are frequently away from home for substantial durations. Young girls are introduced to household chores early in life, while boys enjoy more excellent leisure and playtime. Boys typically undergo initiation ceremonies between the ages of seven and nine. These ceremonies, presided over by the lama, involve feasting and drinking.

Sherpa Weddings and Funerals:

Sherpa weddings, or 'zendi,' are vibrant celebrations marked by cultural traditions. Adorned in their finest attire, the groom's family embarks on a procession to the bride's home. There, they are regaled with food and drink and reciprocate with dance and song. The festivities extend for a day and night before the bridal party returns home. The marriage is solemnised by applying a mark of butter on the foreheads of the bride and groom. The bride receives a dowry from family and friends, typically rugs, woollen carpets, yak-wool mats, and sometimes cattle.

The Sherpa community observes a series of rituals in the event of a death. The deceased is bathed and shrouded in white. The lama snips a lock of hair from the corpse, facilitating the departure of the life breath (pran). Religious texts are recited, and the lama determines whether the deceased should be buried, cremated, or given a water burial. The lama also decides the timing of the body's removal, which may not occur for several days. During the funeral procession, flags flutter, novice lamas blow conch shells, and drums and cymbals resound. After death, the family conducts rites for the departed and cleanses the home through ritual purification. Sherpas believe that the soul lingers near the house for forty-nine days, culminating in a grand feast on the final day to complete the funeral rites.

The Sherpa Faith:

The Sherpa people adhere to the Nyingmapa sect of Buddhism, the oldest Buddhist sect in Tibet. This tradition emphasises mysticism and incorporates shamanistic elements and local deities borrowed from the pre-Buddhist Bon religion. Alongside Buddha and the primary Buddhist deities, the Sherpa pantheon includes numerous gods and demons believed to inhabit mountains, caves, and forests. These entities must be appeased or venerated through time-honoured rituals integrated into Buddhist practice. Drawing a clear distinction between Bon practices and Buddhism in Sherpa culture is often challenging.

Guardians of Sacred Mountains:

Many of the towering Himalayan peaks are revered as divine entities. For instance, Sherpas refer to Mount Everest as 'Chomolungma,' the 'Mother of the World,' worshipping it as a sacred deity. Mount Makalu is revered as the deity Shankar, equated with Shiva in Hinduism. Each clan recognises mountain gods associated with specific peaks as protective deities.

Spiritual Leaders and Practices:

The Sherpa's day-to-day religious affairs are overseen by lamas, who are often married and lead a domestic life. These village lamas preside over ceremonies and rituals. Additionally, shamans (lhawa) and soothsayers (mindung) play vital roles in supernatural matters and the spirit realm. They identify witches (pem), act as conduits for gods and spirits, and diagnose illnesses.

The Role of Monasteries:

Monasteries, or 'gompa,' are distinctive in Sherpa culture. The Solu-Khumbu region alone boasts approximately two dozen of these monastic institutions. These monasteries house communities of lamas or monks (sometimes nuns) who pledge celibacy and lead lives dedicated to introspection and religious enlightenment. The community significantly respects and supports them. Their interactions with the outside world are limited to annual festivals, open to the public, and reciting sacred texts at funerals.

The Legend of the Yeti:

Within Sherpa folklore, there exists a captivating legend—stories of the Yeti, often referred to in the West as the 'Abominable Snowman' or 'Bigfoot.' According to one story, the Yetis roamed in far greater numbers, terrorising local villages. The elders devised a plan to eliminate this menace. They assembled in a high alpine pasture, each bearing a large kettle of 'chāng' (maize beer) and weapons such as sticks, knives, and swords. Simulating inebriation, they began to 'fight' amongst themselves. As evening descended, the villagers returned to their homes, leaving behind their weapons and copious amounts of beer. Hidden in the mountains, the Yetis observed these proceedings and descended upon the pasture upon the villagers' departure. They consumed the remaining beer and, intoxicated, turned upon each other. By night's end, most of the Yetis had perished. A few of the less inebriated survivors escaped, vowing revenge. Nevertheless, their dwindling numbers compelled them to retreat to remote mountain caves, where they would remain hidden from human discovery. On rare occasions, they re-emerge to confront humans. Such is the legend.

The Sherpa culture is a rich tapestry, intricately woven over centuries of high-altitude living, mystical traditions, and the profound influence of Buddhism and shamanistic practices. Their story is of resilience, reverence for nature, and harmonious coexistence with the majestic Himalayas. As we journey through Pemba Gelje Sherpa's life, we must remember that his identity is deeply rooted in this captivating cultural backdrop, for it is the crucible from which he emerged—a faithful Sherpa.

Smiling faces, and a lady of wisdom

Heavy load, and a place called home

The faces of life

Pemba, Gelje Sherpa in traditional costume.

CHAPTER 1
THE CALL OF
THE MOUNTAINS

To truly understand the Sherpas, one must first grasp the historical significance of their land, nestled in the shadow of the mighty Himalayas. Pemba Gelje Sherpa, my biographical subject and a revered Sherpa mountaineer, has told me the stories passed down through generations. These stories speak of people who have inhabited the unforgiving terrain for centuries, built their lives around the mountains, and have become synonymous with the art of climbing.

The Sherpas' connection to the mountains is deep-rooted, an inextricable bond forged through years of toil, respect, and spirituality. They have an innate understanding of the Himalayas, knowing its treacherous turns and icy crevices like the lines on the palms of their calloused hands. Mountain climbing is second nature to them, as they have spent their lives traversing the formidable peaks and navigating the unpredictable weather conditions that haunt these majestic summits.

The Sherpa legacy is not solely limited to mountaineering prowess, though it is undeniably a crucial aspect of their heritage. It encompasses an intricate tapestry of traditions, rituals, and customs passed down through the ages. Their resilient spirit, unwavering commitment to their community, and unmatched humility have become a hallmark of the Sherpa people.

During my research, I have observed their rituals up close, witnessing the power of prayer flags fluttering in the wind and sending blessings to the mountains and all those who dare to challenge their might. I have marvelled at the sight of the Sherpas, their step sure-footed faces filled with calm determination as they carry immense loads up treacherous terrain, supporting climbers who dare to challenge the limits of human endurance.

Pemba Gelje Sherpa has guided me throughout this incredible exploration into the Sherpa legacy. He has shared with me the intricacies of their spiritual practices, recounting how the mountain gods are appeased through sacred ceremonies, ensuring the safety of all those who venture into the realm of the peaks.

But it is not just their spiritual connection that sets the Sherpas apart. Their unwavering loyalty to mountaineering clients, unparalleled skill in guiding climbers through treacherous routes, and exceptional ability to adapt to harsh environments have made them an integral part of mountain exploration. Without the support and expertise of the Sherpas, many towering summits would remain unconquered, and the stories of daring triumphs would remain untold.

Reflecting on the Sherpa legacy, I am astounded by their resilience and indomitable spirit. Their commitment to their craft, unwavering resolve, and unyielding dedication to their community inspire awe and admiration. The Sherpas are not just climbers; they embody a life intertwined with the mountains—living, breathing testaments to the Sherpa legacy.

In the following chapters of 'Step by Step,' I will delve deeper into the stories that make up this remarkable Sherpa legacy. Through Pemba Gelje's experiences and those of his fellow climbers, we will uncover the triumphs, tragedies, and unbreakable bonds that have shaped the Sherpa people and left an indelible mark on mountaineering.

A Glimpse Into Pemba Gelje's Childhood:

Recounting Pemba Gelje's upbringing in a small Sherpa village was like peering into a world untouched by time. Nestled amidst the Himalayan peaks, the village of Kharikhola was a tight-knit community where traditions flourished and nature commanded the utmost respect.

Pemba Gelje's family lived in a modest house crafted from sturdy stones and timber, its walls steeped in the stories of generations past. Flickering firelight illuminated his parents' faces as they regaled him with tales of legendary climbers and fearless adventurers, igniting a spark within him.

Life in the village was far from easy. Survival depended on taming the unforgiving terrain and braving the harsh elements. From a young age, Pemba was taught the art of resilience, honing his skills in navigating treacherous trails and enduring bone-chilling cold. He learned to traverse the icy slopes as a Yak herder, his small frame defying gravity as he later followed in the footsteps of seasoned mountaineers. Though he was a child, the grit and determination that pulsated through his veins gave him an edge beyond his tender years.

He summarised his childhood for me in his own words:

'Living with my parents in our village home was typical for a little Sherpa kid. I was mostly with my mom in the gardens while in the village. I also spent significant time in the "goths" makeshift sheds in the high-altitude pasture above our village, where my parents shifted our yaks and cows. Traditionally, Sherpas took their cattle to higher grounds in spring, where lush nutrient grasses are abundant. At the age of 9, I was sent to the monastery by my parents to study Buddhism and become a monk. It was common practice for a Sherpa family enduring hardship to send their kids to the monastery where they get free education, food and shelter. In a way, it was a way out of poverty for something better in life. Growing up in a big family is hard, and I grew up in a family of 9 siblings. Food was scarce back then, and we only got to eat rice once or twice a year during festivities.'

Despite his hardships, signs of Pemba Gelje's passion for climbing were evident from the outset. He would often disappear into the surrounding mountains, scaling rocky cliffs with a fearlessness that belied his age. Pemba Gelje's unwavering enthusiasm was matched only by his insatiable curiosity. He would sit for hours, studying maps and planning imaginary expeditions, fueled by an insatiable hunger for exploration.

The village elders recognised the fire burning within Pemba and nurtured his spirit for adventure. They guided him through the intricacies of mountaineering techniques, imparting their invaluable wisdom. Eager to learn, Pemba absorbed every detail with an unquenchable thirst for knowledge. His tiny hands grew accustomed to gripping ropes, and his bare feet danced across treacherous paths, always searching for the next challenge.

As Pemba blossomed into adolescence, his passion for climbing intensified. He began accompanying seasoned mountaineers on expeditions, serving as a cook and climbing Sherpa assistant, and absorbing every intrepid experience like a sponge. The arduous treks, the roaring winds, and the breathtaking vistas solidified his determination to conquer the world's most formidable peaks.

During those formative years, Pemba Gelje's resilience, forged in the crucible of his childhood, laid the bedrock for his future triumphs. Through trials and tribulations, he learned to overcome adversity and face the unknown with unwavering courage. His village provided the nurturing soil that allowed his love for mountaineering to take root and flourish.

In recounting Pemba Gelje Sherpa's childhood, one cannot overlook its profound impact on his character. His humble beginnings, the challenges he encountered, and his unyielding passion for climbing created the man poised to become a legendary figure in the mountaineering world.

The Mountain's Call:

Delving into the moment, Pemba felt the irresistible pull of the mountains, the allure of the unknown, and the drive to conquer the highest peaks was like embarking on a journey into the deepest recesses of the human spirit. As a biographer and author, it was my duty to unravel the layers of Pemba Gelje Sherpa's soul and offer readers a glimpse of his profound connection with the mountains.

I spent countless hours speaking with Pemba, listening intently to his words while simultaneously observing the depths of his emotions. Each sentence he said seemed to carry a weight that transcended the realm of language. It was as if Pemba was reliving his most treasured memories, his eyes betraying a sense of exhilaration mixed with the solemnity that only a mountain enthusiast could understand.

Pemba Gelje's journey into mountaineering began in his childhood village nestled amidst the towering Himalayas. Surrounded by the majesty of the peaks, it was impossible to ignore their siren call. He spoke of waking up to the crisp mountain air, the distant echoes of avalanches, and the sight of sun-kissed peaks piercing through the morning mist. Growing up amidst such grandeur, it was no surprise that the mountains imprinted themselves deep within Pemba Gelje's being.

But in a single moment, a seismic shift in Pemba Gelje's life would forever bind him to the mountains. It was during a shift as a kitchen boy in Lukla when, by sheer chance, he saw a documentary showcasing climbers battling against the elements on the formidable Everest. As Pemba watched, a fire ignited an insatiable yearning to confront the challenges ahead. The intensity and determination etched on the climbers' faces resonated deeply with Pemba, awakening within him a desire he could not quell.

From that day forward, Pemba embarked on a relentless pursuit of mountaineering knowledge. He voraciously devoured books and articles, hounded local climbers with endless questions, and made it his mission to glean every morsel of information about the unforgiving world that awaited him. His dedication was unmatched, his hunger insatiable, and it became increasingly clear that the mountains had claimed him as their own.

Pemba Gelje's first expedition, a modest trek to the town of Namche Bazar, carrying food supplies as a porter, was a baptism of fire. The biting cold, thin air, and unforgiving terrain tested his physical and mental endurance. But with each arduous step, his passion for mountaineering deepened. Pemba found solace in the untamed wildness of the mountains, a state of mind that transcended the mundane and awakened a primal connection with the natural world.

This connection, intertwined with Pemba Gelje's unyielding determination, propelled him to tackle the world's highest peaks. The allure of the unknown became an irresistible force, beckoning him towards uncharted territories and testing his limits. Pemba Gelje's conquest of these colossal summits was not merely an act of human triumph but a testament to the indomitable spirit that resided within him, nurtured by the mountains.

Delving into the moment, Pemba felt the irresistible pull of the mountains, the allure of the unknown, and the drive to conquer the highest peaks meant unravelling the very essence of his being. As I chronicled his journey, I couldn't help but be enthralled by the magnitude of the mountains' call on Pemba Gelje Sherpa. This was not a mere obsession or a hobby but a sincere devotion, a spiritual bond that transcended ordinary human existence.

I realised then that the mountains had chosen Pemba rather than vice versa. They had sensed within him an unquenchable thirst for adventure, a hunger for the untamed, and a willingness to sacrifice everything to glimpse their awe-inspiring grandeur. Through Pemba Gelje's eyes, I, too, felt the call of the mountains, their ethereal beauty and unconquerable challenges, an ever-present presence in my mind.

And so, I continued my task as Pemba Gelje's biographer, delving deeper into his story, chronicling the moments when he scaled unimaginable heights and pushed the boundaries of human capability. In the following pages, I would recount the triumphs and tragedies, the moments of serenity and despair, as Pemba Gelje Sherpa heeded The Mountain's Call and embarked on a journey that would forever define him as one of the world's best mountain guides.

Pemba Gelje Sherpa, where he feels most at home, in the mountains.

CHAPTER 2
A STUDENT MONK

At the tender age of nine, a time in a young Sherpa boy's life equivalent to what might be deemed adulthood in the Western world, your fate led you to the sacred confines of a monastery. Your parents, driven by the harsh realities of life in the unforgiving mountains, made the difficult choice to send you there, cloaked in the guise of education. As you would later discover, the motivations ran deeper; they were borne out of a dire struggle for sustenance that had left your family at the precipice of survival. In the time-honoured tradition of Sherpa families facing such adversity, their children sought refuge in the monastic life.

Guided by an uncle, a respected Lama in his own right, Pemba embarked on this transformative journey. The uncle pledged to Pemba Gelje's mother to watch over him, ensuring his well-being. In their flowing robes and wisdom, the monks bestowed upon him the vestments of a monk and ceremoniously shaved his head.

Life within the monastery unfolded for Pemba according to a strict monastic code, a tapestry woven from the revered teachings of the Lamas. Deviation from these sacred precepts spelt inevitable punishment, often a meandering walk around the monastery with a small bag of rocks. Each circuit saw the transfer of a stone to the elder Lama. Rare were the occasions when you could venture beyond the monastery's hallowed walls; typically, such excursions were reserved for family emergencies or escorted gatherings to collect alms and sustenance.

According to his recollection, Pemba recalls the days blurring into an almost monotonous continuum of prayers and scripture studies, interspersed with fleeting moments of respite. The rhythm of monastic life, a steadfast pulse, echoed through every corner of the sacred institution.

As a novice or a mature member, your day they were adhered to a fixed schedule. You stirred at the resounding call of 4:30 AM, a summons unbound by the constraints of Saturdays or Sundays. An hour-long assembly in the temple commenced voices in unison to recite mantras. Personal hygiene rituals unfolded at the fountains scattered about the monastery, showers a foreign concept. At precisely 6:30 AM, monks gathered neatly before the gate, and the journey beyond began,

barefooted through the adjacent village to solicit alms of sustenance. The return to the monastery transpired at 7:30 AM, and the day's first meal consisted of whatever the town had bestowed (those with surplus offerings sharing with others).

From 8:30 AM to 11:30 AM, novice monks engrossed themselves in pursuing knowledge. The sole meal of the day was served, and from then on, no morsel would grace your lips until the following morning's breakfast. In the afternoon, they brought a return to academic endeavours, continuing until 5:30 PM. Gathered in the temple by 7 PM, prayers held sway, and all were in their beds by nightfall.

Amidst the peaceful night hours, Pemba shared that your thoughts often ventured beyond the monastery's cloistered walls. A restless curiosity dwelled within you, akin to a caged bird yearning to take flight. Yet, you remained composed, nurturing the knowledge that you would someday venture to experience the world beyond.

'When you reached the age of fourteen, after five years as a Lama, a profound transformation stirred within you. One dawn, as the sun cast its golden rays across the sky, an inexplicable awakening transpired. The vibrant orange hues of daybreak found you sleepless, your thoughts ensnared by the distant memories of home. You pondered your parents' well-being and their shelter's safety with its leaky "Khar" grass roof. Your thoughts wandered to your brothers, their lives unfolding far from your watchful eyes. It was as though the mountains that cradled you called out your name.' He told me.

He explained how he eventually decided to leave—the time had come for him to take flight. 'A yearning swelled within me, and the decision was made. With the first rays of dawn, I embarked on a quest, my feet setting a relentless pace toward Lukla. There were no missions for the monastery no food collections to undertake. I possessed nothing save for the robes that clung to my body. I had absconded, run away from the monastic life, and there was a wry smile on my face, as I recall. I was acutely aware of the wrongness of my actions, yet the exhilarating taste of freedom was equally apparent. As I walked, I pondered what lay ahead, aware that the elders would soon discover my absence and set forth to retrieve me. Yet, my spirit was steadfast, my resolve unshaken. It was time to forge my path to earn a livelihood to support my family. The monastery had imparted invaluable lessons, grounding me, nurturing me, and fostering inner peace. Yet, another spirit now stirred within me, the spirit of adventure. I wondered where this newfound journey would lead.'

Pemba, aged 9, at the Pangom Tashi Sanga Choling monastery in Katmandu, Nepal.

Departing the monastery marked the inception of a life filled with boundless adventures for Pemba.

A monastery possesses the power to unveil the deepest wells of wisdom. There, amidst its sacred halls, Pemba gleaned the essence of prayer and patience, two virtues that would later define his life as a mountaineer. The monastery also served as a sanctuary for lessons that he would draw upon.

Pemba Gelje's brother Pemba Pemba Chongba, aged 15.
At the Pangom Tashi Sanga Choling monastery,
Katmandu, Nepal.

CHAPTER 3
A SHERPA'S PATH

With his wealth of experience and innate understanding of the mountains, Pemba seemed to possess an otherworldly connection to this place. He could hear the Summit's siren song, a melody that only a select few would ever truly comprehend. The mountains were calling, and their call was impossible to resist.

During our breaks along the trail, as we sat silently, admiring the landscape's exquisite beauty, Pemba began to share his journey with me. His voice was filled with nostalgia and reverence, his words carrying the weight of a thousand stories.

He spoke of his first encounter with these majestic peaks, a young boy filled with wonder and curiosity. When he laid eyes on Everest, he knew he was destined to explore its heights, stand atop its summit, and embrace the world from a place few would ever reach.

With each step he took along the trail, his passion grew more robust, his determination unwavering. He spoke of his sacrifices and hardships, all in pursuit of a dream that seemed impossible to many. But Pemba was not one to be deterred by the doubts of others. He understood that the mountains demanded respect but rewarded those who dared to challenge them.

Pemba Gelje's stories became more vivid and captivating as we continued our trek. He recounted his encounters with avalanches and blizzards, moments that tested his resolve and pushed him to his limits. And yet, through it all, he remained steadfast, his spirit unyielding in the face of adversity.

He spoke of the camaraderie among climbers, the bond that forms in the harshest conditions. These individuals, united by a shared love for the mountains, became a family, supporting and encouraging each other every step of the way. It was a brotherhood forged in the crucible of the highest peaks, where trust and reliance on one another were paramount.

But as Pemba delved deeper into his stories, a sombre tone crept into his voice. He spoke of those who had lost their lives on the mountain, their dreams cut short, their spirits forever entwined with the unforgiving slopes. For every triumph, there were moments of tragedy, reminders of the immense power and unpredictability of the mountains.

Listening to his words, I began to understand the allure, the magnetic pull that drew individuals to these treacherous heights. It was more than just a desire for personal achievement; it was a pursuit of something greater, a quest for meaning and enlightenment. The summit of Everest held a mystique that could not be put into words, a mystical energy that infused the air and awakened the soul. Much like surfers look for the perfect wave and draw upon the life force, mountaineers seek the ideal peak.

The Summit's siren song echoed my thoughts long after Pemba finished speaking. It called to me, tempting me with its promises of discovery and transformation. And though I knew that I would never attempt to climb Everest myself, I couldn't help but be drawn into its orbit, forever changed by the stories that unfolded before me.

At that moment, I realised that the true essence of Pemba Gelje's biography extended far beyond his achievements. It was a testament to the indomitable spirit of the human race, the unyielding pursuit of our limits. It was a celebration of the mountains, the guardians of the world, enchanting and elusive, forever captivating the hearts and minds of those who dared to listen to their song. And as I continued to write, I knew I was privileged to be part of this remarkable journey, forever bound to the magic of the mountains.

A Client Recount. Navigating the Icefall:

'As we approached the icefall, the air grew heavy with anticipation, each of us acutely aware of the risks ahead. With his unwavering confidence and years of experience, Pemba led the way, his footsteps marking the path through the treacherous maze. The ice crunched beneath our crampons, reverberating through the silent, frozen landscape.

I watched in awe as Pemba manoeuvred across the ever-shifting terrain, his agility and familiarity with the icefall apparent in every step. It was like he danced with the elements, defying gravity and mastering the chaos. He knew when to step lightly, delicately probing the ice for stability, and when to leap, trusting his instincts to carry him across the gaping crevasses.

The challenge's sheer scale became apparent as we ventured deeper into the icefall's heart. Towering seracs loomed above us, their jagged edges threatening to collapse at any moment. Pemba Gelje's eyes remained fixed on the path ahead, his focus unyielding, his senses heightened to the slightest hint of danger.

We progressed slowly but steadily, weaving our way through the icy labyrinth. Each step required careful consideration, a calculated move to avoid the hidden dangers beneath the surface. The constant threat of avalanches hung over us like a dark cloud, a reminder that the icefall held no mercy for those who dared to underestimate it.

Time seemed to lose all meaning as we pressed on, the relentless cold seeping into our bones. The icy winds whipped around us, biting at our exposed skin as if mocking our audacity to challenge this harsh and unforgiving environment. Yet, Pemba Gelje's unwavering determination and resilience inspired us to persevere.

At times, the icefall seemed to conspire against us, shifting and collapsing with an almost malicious intent. But Pemba anticipated these treacherous moments, guiding us with an intuition born from countless journeys through this frozen wilderness. His knowledge of the icefall was not mere familiarity; it was a deep understanding, an intimate connection with the very soul of the mountain.

And then, after what felt like an eternal struggle, we emerged from the icefall, greeted by the crisp mountain air and the sight of the vast Khumbu Glacier sprawling before us. We stood in awe of what we had accomplished, humbled by the sheer power of nature and our resilience.

As we continued our trek back towards Everest Base Camp, the memory of navigating the icefall lingered in my mind. It was a testament to the indomitable spirit of the Sherpas, their remarkable ability to tame the untameable, and their unwavering dedication to their craft. With his infectious smile and unyielding determination, Pemba had shown me what it truly meant to be a mountaineer to conquer not only the physical challenges but also the inner demons that lurked within.'

When I heard this account of a climb from one of his clients, I knew that my role as Pemba Gelje's author went beyond just recording his remarkable journey. It was a privilege to bear witness to his indomitable spirit, share in his triumphs and tribulations, and strive to capture this extraordinary man's essence in the pages of his biography. And so, with renewed purpose and deep gratitude for the experiences ahead, I vowed to continue this journey step by step.

Sherpa Strong:

I learned that you must delve into their rich historical timeline to understand the essence of Sherpa's strength. The Sherpas have long inhabited the mountainous regions of Nepal, primarily settling in the Solu-Khumbu region, where the majestic Everest stands as a towering testament to their indomitable spirit.

For generations, Sherpas have relied on their intimate knowledge of the land, passed down through oral tradition, to navigate the formidable Himalayan peaks. Their unique physiology, adapted to high-altitude environments, gives them a distinct advantage over others in these extreme conditions. However, their unbreakable willpower and mental fortitude set them apart as true mountain warriors.

Sherpa tribes were originally Tibetan nomads who migrated to the Khumbu valley in the 14th century. From humble beginnings, they lived in this harsh and unforgiving terrain, relying on subsistence agriculture and trading goods between Tibet and Nepal. They adapted to the mountainous lifestyle with time, becoming expert climbers and guides.

The British first recognised the strength of the Sherpas during their early expeditions to Everest in the early 20th century. The Sherpas served as invaluable guides and porters, allowing these pioneering mountaineers to achieve what was once thought impossible. Their immense physical strength and innate knowledge of the mountains paved the way for Everest's conquest and modern mountaineering's birth.

But Sherpa's strength extends far beyond the physical realm. It reflects their deep spiritual connection to the mountains and their unwavering determination to protect and honour the sacredness of these peaks. For the Sherpas, mountains are not merely geographical formations; they are revered as deities, and each expedition is undertaken with utmost respect and reverence.

Sherpa's strength is also interwoven with a profound sense of community and solidarity. They work together as a tightly knit unit, supporting and uplifting one another, even in the face of unimaginable challenges. This collective spirit enables them to overcome obstacles that would break the resolve of most individuals. Sherpa vital means being selfless, putting the group's needs before one's own, and recognising the interconnectedness of all beings.

My journey with Pemba has taught me that Sherpa's strength is not just about physical prowess or conquering mountains. It is a holistic embodiment of resilience, humility, and an unyielding spirit from centuries of navigating the problematic Himalayan landscapes. Their strength lies not only in their bodies but also in their hearts and minds.

As I delve deeper into Pemba Gelje's life story, I am driven by a newfound appreciation for his immense strength as an individual and a representative of the Sherpa people. Through his experiences, I hope to shed light on the power of the human spirit and the extraordinary capabilities within each of us, waiting to be awakened.

Sherpa strong is not a mere catchphrase but a testament to the undying spirit of these remarkable individuals who have defied the odds and risen above the highest peaks. It invites us all to tap into our reservoirs of strength and resilience, confront the challenges that lay before us, and embrace the indomitable spirit of the Sherpas as a guiding light on our journeys.

Two Grateful clients

CHAPTER 4
A MOMENT OF
INNER REFLECTION

As we ventured deeper into the heart of the Khumbu region, Pemba Gelje's eyes shone with anticipation and nostalgia. He had spent a lifetime exploring these mountains, guiding countless climbers to the summit of Everest. But something more lay beyond the summit for him, beyond the physical challenge and personal achievement.

Pemba shared his deepest motivations with me during one of our acclimatisation stops. We were perched on a rocky outcrop overlooking a vast valley with prayer flags fluttering in the wind. He took a deep breath, his voice tinged with melancholy and recounted his journey.

'For me, the mountains have always been a place of solace and rejuvenation,' Pemba began, his gaze fixed on the swirling mist that hid the peaks. 'They have taught me so much about resilience, perseverance, and the power of the human spirit. But there is also a deeper connec-tion, a spiritual calling that beckons me beyond the summit.'

He explained how the mountains had become a conduit for self-discovery and growth, not just for himself but all those who ventured into their unforgiving embrace. Pemba believed that climbing Everest was not just about conquering a physical challenge or obtaining a prestigious title; it was about transcending one's limitations and finding a deeper purpose in life.

'As climbers, we push ourselves to the limits of human endurance, facing the harshest elements and battling our inner demons,' Pemba said, his voice filled with conviction. 'But it is in those moments of struggle, when everything seems impossible, that we truly discover who we are and what we are capable of.'

He spoke of the countless trekkers and climbers he had guided up the treacherous slopes of Everest, watching as they transformed before his eyes. Many came to the mountains seeking personal glory or an escape from their everyday lives, but they left with a newfound sense of humility, gratitude, and reverence for the world around them.

'There is a beauty in the mountains that goes beyond mere aesthetics,' Pemba mused, his words carrying the weight of years of experience. 'It is a beauty that connects us to something greater than ourselves, a force that reminds us of our place in the grand tapestry of life.'

As Pemba descended into the depths of his introspection, I felt a surge of awe and admiration for the man sitting beside me. Here was a man who had scaled the highest peaks on earth, faced death and triumphed, yet remained humble, grounded, and committed to sharing his experiences with the world.

At that moment, I realised that Pemba Gelje's story was not just a story of mountaineering feats and daring adventures but a testament to the human spirit and our innate capacity for growth and transformation. Beyond the summit of Everest, Pemba had discovered a profound truth - that the mountains are not just a physical realm to be conquered but a spiritual realm that holds the power to shape and nurture the soul.

With each step we took, as the air grew thinner and colder, I felt a sense of purpose and determination ignite within me. Pemba opened my eyes to a new understanding of the world and a deeper appreciation for the magic and majesty of the mountains. And I knew that together, we would bring his incredible story to life and perhaps, in doing so, offer a glimpse of the immense power and beauty that lies beyond the summit.

Pemba loves to guide his clients safely on treks and climbs. Always prepared, constantly aware, and always places safety over ego.

CHAPTER 5
SHERPA BROTHERHOOD

The concept of the Sherpa Brotherhood transcended mere familial bonds; it was an intricate web of interwoven lives, held together by unbreakable threads of trust and love. To truly understand this brotherhood, one had to witness it in action, and there was no better place to do so than amidst the soaring peaks of the Himalayas.

As we trekked along the arduous path towards Everest Base Camp, I observed how the Sherpas supported one another physically and emotionally. It was not just the heavy loads they carried on their backs but also the burdens they bore within their hearts. Each seemed to have an innate understanding of the struggles and triumphs their fellow Sherpas faced, and they approached their collective journey with unwavering solidarity.

In the moments of exhaustion, when fatigue threatened to consume their spirits, their bond pulled them through. Whether it was a gentle pat on the back or a shared laugh, they lifted each other, reminding one another of their shared purpose and the indomitable spirit of the Sherpa people.

It was as if their very existence was intertwined, each life connected to the other in a dance of strength and resilience. Their unity was not born out of necessity alone but of a deep respect for one another's sacrifices and dedication. Every step they took, every breath they exhaled, was a testament to their unwavering commitment to their Sherpa kin.

Watching Pemba interact with his fellow Sherpas was a revelation in itself. He was not just their leader but a friend, a mentor, and a confidant. They sought his guidance in times of uncertainty and looked up to him with unwavering trust. Pemba, in turn, never hesitated to lend a helping hand or share a word of encouragement. He epitomised the selflessness that defined the Sherpa Brotherhood.

Within this brotherhood, the Sherpas found strength and solace, a sanctuary against the ever-changing landscape of the mountains. They celebrated one another's triumphs, mourned each other's losses, and navigated the unforgiving terrain that nature threw their way together.

Pemba in his home village of Kharikhola.

To them, the mountains were not just impenetrable barriers or majestic landscapes; they were living, breathing entities that demanded their utmost respect. And as they moved through these sacred peaks, their spirit of camaraderie grew more muscular, their bond deepening with every obstacle they conquered.

In witnessing the Sherpa Brotherhood, I couldn't help but be moved by the selflessness and compassion that flowed effortlessly between them. It was a reminder that true strength lies not just in individual achievements but in the collective support of a community.

In capturing this essence within the pages of Pemba Gelje's autobiography, I hoped to pay tribute to the unbreakable bond that united the Sherpa people. Their story, woven with threads of love, sacrifice, and resilience, was a testament to human connection's power and the Sherpa Brotherhood's beauty.

CHAPTER 6
A MOUNTAIN'S LESSON

As our treacherous path wound through the majestic yet unforgiving terrain, I struggled to keep pace with the resilient Sherpa. Each step I took felt like a monumental accomplishment, a fleeting victory in the face of immense hardship. Yet Pemba, with his unwavering smile and quiet strength, effortlessly guided me through the treacherous landscape as if it were second nature to him.

During one particularly gruelling ascent, the true lesson of the mountains revealed itself to me. We had been climbing for hours, our bodies weary and our spirits tested. With every step, the air grew thinner, seemingly stealing the breath from our lungs. The backpack's weight pressing against my shoulders intensified, threatening to drag me back to the valley below. Doubt began to seep into my thoughts, whispering stories of defeat and urging me to turn around.

But Pemba, with his calm demeanour, persisted. He knew that the mountains demanded physical strength and mental fortitude. He urged me to focus on the small victories—the crunch of gravel beneath our boots, the rhythmic sound of our breaths intertwining, the serenity of the untouched landscape stretching out before us. He reminded me that the mountains were conquerable obstacles and influential teachers.

In the face of adversity, the mountains taught us patience. Every step had to be deliberate, careful, and deliberate, mirroring life's slow and intentional nature. The mountains taught us humility, humbling us in the face of their majestic grandeur and reminding us of our tiny place in the vast universe. They taught us resilience as we persevered through the biting wind, bone-chilling cold, and sheer exhaustion. And above all, the mountains taught us to trust—in ourselves, each other, and the journey that lay before us.

As we reached the summit, thin and sharp air, I looked at the panoramic vista before me and felt a profound sense of accomplishment. With their towering peaks and treacherous slopes, the mountains feasted on our determination and rewarded us with a breathtaking view reserved only for those willing to endure. I knew then that this journey was not just about Pemba Gelje's story—it was about humanity's enduring spirit and our ability to conquer literal and metaphorical mountains.

From that moment on, I approached my role as Pemba Gelje's ghost-writer with a newfound appreciation for the power of storytelling. Pemba Gelje's biography was not just a collection of words on a page but a testament to the indomitable human spirit and the lessons we learn from our most formidable challenges. In the grand tapestry of life, each thread is woven with purpose, connecting us to our shared humanity and reminding us of the strength that lies within us all.

As I closed my eyes that night, the memory of the mountain's lesson seeped into my dreams, reassuring me that our journey had only just begun. With Pemba by my side, his unwavering smile lighting our path, I knew we would navigate the peaks and valleys of his extraordinary life together. And as I continued to walk this winding road, I carried with me the wisdom of the mountains, etching their lessons deep within my heart.

The Unforgiving Storm:

It was a crisp morning when the storm began to brew. The wind whipped through the valleys, carrying an eerie sense of foreboding. Pemba Gelje's face, usually adorned with a warm smile, now looked concerned as he studied the clouds gathering in the distance. Instinctively, he tightened his grip on his trekking poles, fully aware of the upcoming challenge.

The storm cells grew more aggressive as the day progressed, unleashing their fury upon the mountain. Snowflakes swirled and danced in the air, the biting cold seeping into every fibre of our being. Visibility rapidly deteriorated, reducing our surroundings to ghostly shadows. The once vibrant landscape now transformed into a desolate, frozen wasteland.

With his years of experience and intimate knowledge of these mountains, Pemba took charge. He guided our group with unwavering confidence, his steps calculated and deliberate. Communication was reduced to the solemn sound of our breathing and the occasional shout to stay close. The storm's deafening roar drowned out any attempts at conversation.

With each passing moment, the storm intensified. The wind howled like a beast hungry for prey, relentlessly shaking our bodies and testing our resolve. We huddled close together, seeking solace and strength in our shared determination to survive. Pemba, ever the beacon of hope, urged us forward despite the overwhelming odds stacked against us.

The snowfall grew heavier, blanketing the trails and obscuring our path. The once familiar route became an intricate maze, navigated only by Pemba Gelje's unwavering intuition and years of traversing these unforgiving terrains. We trudged onward, each step a battle against the elements; our senses strained as we fought to make out the elusive markers amidst the whiteout.

Hours turned into eternities as we pushed through the storm, the relentless assault of snow and wind threatening to break our spirits. Pemba Gelje's true character shone through in these moments of despair. His unwavering determination became contagious, spreading like wildfire amongst the weary group. His words of encouragement echoed in our ears, a reminder of the strength within each of us.

Against all odds, we persevered and finally made shelter in our tents. Pemba made sure everyone had pitched theirs before he took care of his own. The storm howled outside, hinting at the immense power it still possessed. While grateful for shelter, we knew our battle with the elements was far from over. But I felt hope as I looked around at my fellow climbers' exhausted yet resolute faces and Pemba Gelje's calm and comforting presence.

The storm eventually passed, but its impact remained etched in our memories. It was during those harrowing hours that Pemba Gelje's true strength and character were unveiled. His unwavering dedication to his craft and steadfast commitment to those he guided were awe-inspiring.

The storm's aftermath lay before us as we emerged from the tents. The landscape, once concealed under a blanket of snow, now shimmered in the soft glow of the rising sun. Our hearts, still pounding with the adrenaline of survival, were filled with gratitude and reverence for the mountains that had tested us and the Sherpa who had led us through the storm.

The unforgiving storm had brought us to our knees, but it was in that vulnerability that we discovered our true strength. The remarkable journey through both triumph and adversity humbled us.

As we trekked further into the heart of the Himalayas, I watched Pemba face numerous challenges with unwavering determination. The biting cold winds that clawed at our skin, the steep and treacherous paths that tested our every step, and the thinning air that made breathing laborious – none of these obstacles seemed to dampen Pemba Gelje's spirits. It seemed to invigorate him, fueling his passion for the mountains he called home.

I remember one particular moment when a fierce snowstorm blanketed the trail, transforming the landscape into an ethereal wonderland. Most people would have sought refuge, waiting for the storm to pass, but not Pemba. With an almost childlike excitement, he led the way, his footsteps leaving a trail in the freshly fallen snow. He revelled in the challenge, every step a testament to his unyielding spirit.

As we trekked higher and higher, the air grew thinner, and the physical strain on our bodies became more pronounced. Yet, Pemba remained steadfast, his spirit unbroken. He effortlessly navigated the steep inclines, his surefootedness a testament to his years of experience in the mountains. His endurance seemed boundless as if his spirit connected him directly to the earth's energy.

But it was not just his physical prowess that impressed me. Pemba Gelje's triumph of the spirit went beyond mere physicality. It was an indomitable will to embrace life's challenges and find beauty in the harshest conditions. It was an unwavering belief that every hurdle and setback could be overcome.

One evening, as we sat huddled around a crackling fire in a Sherpa village, Pemba shared his philosophy of life with me. He spoke of the mountains as a physical and spiritual source of strength and wisdom. He believed that the hills tested the limits of human perseverance, pushing us to confront our fears and insecurities. Pemba saw himself as a conduit between these towering giants and those who sought to conquer them. He said his purpose was to guide and inspire others to discover their triumph of the spirit.

As I listened to his words, I couldn't help but be moved by the sheer depth of his understanding. Pemba Gelje's triumph of the spirit was a personal achievement and a gift he shared with the world. Through his stories, experiences, and unwavering smile, he showed others that the human spirit could overcome any obstacle.

In those few days spent trekking alongside Pemba, I learned that triumph of the spirit is not a destination but a journey. It is the relentless pursuit of personal growth, the unwavering belief in oneself, and the ability to find beauty even in the most challenging circumstances. Pemba embodied all these qualities, and through his presence, he taught me the true meaning of triumph.

As I sit here writing Pemba Gelje's biography, I am inspired by his spirit. His story is one of immense courage, resilience, and unwavering determination. Through the pages of this book, I aim to capture the essence of Pemba Gelje's triumph of the spirit so that others may be inspired to embrace life's challenges with the same unwavering belief in themselves.

The Sherpas have long been the unsung mountaineering heroes, their presence often overshadowed by the towering peaks they navigate with an innate grace. For centuries, they have inhabited the slopes of the Himalayas, climbing these colossal giants as if they were mere hills. It is a legacy rooted in necessity and passion, a testament to this remarkable mountain culture's resilience, strength, and wisdom.

Their rich history stretches back, intertwining with myths and legends of gods and spirits dwelling within these vast mountain ranges. They have been the guardians of these sacred realms, their intrepid souls forged by the formidable challenges they faced amidst the unyielding Himalayan terrain.

Like countless other Sherpas, Pemba Gelje's ancestors were born into lives intricately bound with the mountains. For generations, they have honed their mountaineering skills, adept at navigating treacherous landscapes, traversing icy crevasses, and conquering formidable summits. Their expertise and unwavering commitment have made them trusted companions to explorers and mountaineers worldwide, earning them unparalleled respect and admiration.

But the Sherpas are more than just guides and climbers; they embody mountaineering itself. Their deeply ingrained knowledge of the mountains and ability to connect with the natural world sets them apart. It is an intimate relationship that goes beyond mere physicality and delves into the heart of their culture.

Their legacy is etched into the very fabric of these mountains, their footprints imprinted on the snowy slopes. They have braved blizzards and avalanches, facing peril head-on, with a quiet determination. The Sherpas embody the spirit of the mountains, their unwavering resolve merging with the majestic peaks that have witnessed triumph and tragedy.

Yet, the legacy of the Sherpas extends far beyond mountaineering. Their strength extends to their communities, where they have nurtured a unique culture rooted in unity, compassion, and respect for nature. Their support for one another is unwavering, forming a tight-knit network extending across generations and mountains. With his radiant smile and humble nature, Pemba personifies this sense of community, embodying the very essence of Sherpa culture.

As our journey continued, I couldn't help but be awestruck by the indomitable spirit of the Sherpas. Their legacy is not merely about conquering peaks or scaling heights; it is about preserving a way of life, about cherishing their mountainous home and sharing its wonders with the world. Their impact is immeasurable, and their contribution is imprinted on the annals of mountaineering history.

Throughout the rest of our trek, I would delve deeper into the intricacies of Pemba Gelje's life, capturing the essence of his journey and unveiling the remarkable tapestry of Sherpa culture. Their legacy pulsates through every thread of this captivating narrative, reminding us of the human spirit's resilience and the mountains' transformative power.

In the pages that lay ahead, I would uncover not just the physical challenges that Pemba had faced but also the trials and joys that shaped his character, his unwavering devotion to the mountains, and the endless love he carried for his Sherpa heritage. Together, we would embark on a journey illuminating the rich tapestry of a Sherpa's legacy, forever intertwining our lives amidst the Himalayas' profound beauty and awe-inspiring heights.

CHAPTER 7
BIG BROTHER'S FOOTSTEPS

I have always been captivated by the stories of individuals who embark on daring adventures, challenging the limits of human potential. Pemba Gelje Sherpa's journey was no exception. When his brother, Pemba Chongba, invited him to act as a porter on an Everest ascent, little did Pemba Gelje know that this chapter of his life would be filled with unimaginable hardship and invaluable lessons.

Climbing mountains, regardless of their altitude or terrain, is challenging. Whether scaling a 5,000-meter peak or conquering the daunting heights of an 8,000-meter giant like Everest, dangers lurk at every turn. Seasoned mountaineers understand this all too well, accepting and embracing the risks while doing their best to prepare for them. Yet, it is the hidden dangers that often pose the gravest threats.

This is how Pemba Gelje recalls following in his brother's footsteps:

It was a crisp October morning in 2011 when I found myself standing at the base camp beneath the towering presence of Everest. Pemba Chongba, my brother was a senior Climbing Guide with an esteemed trekking company, had secured me a position as a support staff member responsible for cooking at Everest Camp 2. As I absorbed the magnitude of the opportunity before me, I couldn't help but feel a mix of excitement and trepidation.

Having never ventured into the realm of climbing equipment before, I soon discovered an overwhelming array of tools and gear that would become my companions on this arduous journey. Ice axes, harnesses, crampons, and belay devices were now part of my daily existence, a stark reminder of the challenges ahead. With little time for idle contemplation, I had to quickly adapt and familiarise myself with the intricacies of each item, aware that my lack of expertise could jeopardise my safety and that of the courageous climbers I served.

Pemba Gelje on the roof of the world

Navigating the treacherous Khumbu icefall became a daily routine for me, a task filled with solace and anxiety. The breathtaking beauty of the icy terrain provided reassurance, reminding me of the profound privilege I held to witness such a divine landscape. Yet, the lurking threat of falling into a crevasse served as a constant reminder that danger loomed at every step. I pressed on, driven by a profound sense of purpose and duty, determined to fulfil my role in setting up the Clients' Kitchen, Dining, Shower, and Toilet Tents at Camp 2.

Before diving into the logistical complexities of camp life, I was compelled to participate in an age-old Himalayan tradition. Under the guidance of experienced Sherpas, we built a lhapsu, a traditional rock mound where the gods are believed to convene and bless climbers before they embark on their ascent. It was a solemn affair, the weight of centuries of ritual and spirituality resting on our shoulders. As the monk recited ceremonial prayers and chants, I couldn't help but feel a sense of humility and an overwhelming desire for safe passage through the treacherous paths that lay ahead.

The days melded into nights, and I was physically and mentally tested beyond measure. Everest's harsh, unforgiving conditions demanded resilience from the mountaineers and those like me, who dedicated their efforts to supporting their ambitious pursuit. The frigid winds, the relentless altitude, and the sheer magnitude of the task never ceased to humble me.

Reflecting on those days spent in Big Brother's Footsteps, I realise this journey was about more than just scaling the world's highest peak. It was an initiation into a sacred brotherhood that transcends the bound-aries of blood relations. It taught me the importance of perseverance, humility, and respect for the untamed forces of nature. Above all, it instilled in me a deep appreciation for our shared human experiences, connecting us all to an ancient world of triumph and resilience.

Little did I know that my path would soon diverge from my brother's, unveiling personal trials and triumphs unique to my own story. But for now, as I trudged through the icy terrain, one foot in front of the other,

I knew that our destinies were bound by a shared determination to leave our mark on the unforgiving slopes of Everest.

CHAPTER 8
STEP BY STEP UPON EVEREST

An immutable truth exists in the annals of Himalayan history—a narrative of man's audacity to ascend the Earth's highest realms. The story unfolds above the world's bustling cities and reaches its zenith, where the air thins and the boundaries of human endurance are tested.

Did you know most significant cities sit below 50 meters (164 feet) above sea level? New York and London rest approximately 10 meters (33 feet), while Tokyo and Paris hover around 40 meters (130 feet). Mumbai resides at 20 meters (66 feet), Sydney is below 5 meters (16 feet), and Amsterdam's elevation is paradoxically listed as below 0 meters (0 feet). Yet, in the distant realm of Nepal, perched at around 5,000 meters above sea level, a peculiar city emerges anew each year. This is none other than Everest Base Camp, a tented haven nestled upon a living glacier. Hundreds of brave souls pilgrimage to this altitude-shrouded metropolis every spring. Their ultimate goal: the summit of Mount Everest, the Earth's apex, standing at a staggering 8,848.66 meters (29,031.69 feet) above sea level. Among the populace inhabiting this temporary city, over two-thirds proudly claim Sherpa heritage, an ethnic group indigenous to the Himalayan terrain of Nepal, numbering 150,000 strong.

Fatigue and breathlessness are familiar companions for these fearless souls who converge on Everest's doorstep. At these dizzying altitudes, where oxygen is a precious commodity, breathing becomes a struggle. Yet, amid this thin air, a singular group, the Sherpas, takes centre stage. They, too, ascend the slopes, but their vitality remains undiminished. It's as though the very oxygen they dispense to their clients imbues them with boundless energy. With sinews acclimated to high altitudes and lungs in harmony with rarified air, Sherpas become architects of temporary cities, orchestrators of makeshift kitchens, and tireless transporters of vital supplies. Among their multifaceted roles, some undertake the daunting task of training foreign climbers to navigate treacherous icefalls, communicating their wisdom in fragmented English. As seasoned Sherpa veterans depart Base Camp to secure routes with ropes and ladders, they carry the lifeline of precious oxygen canisters to higher camps. A select few, the elite, meticulously craft ascent strategies as they prepare to guide climbers to the ultimate zenith. Among these distinguished few stands my brother, a Sherpa of unparalleled skill whose unique psychological motivation empowers the climbers under his steadfast guidance.

The Ascent Begins:

The chronicle of my ascent of Everest's formidable summit unfurls here. Standing at the apex, one foot resting in China, the other in Nepal, I faced the relentless Himalayan wind, the icy tendrils I cleared from my oxygen mask. My gaze descended upon the vast expanse of Tibet. In that moment of profound reflection, the curvature of the Earth beneath my boots became a sight of unparalleled significance. I had envisioned this moment for months, pondering the accompanying emotions. Yet, now that I stood atop Mount Everest, the zenith of our world, I found myself curiously devoid of the energy to vocalise my delight, not even within the sanctum of my thoughts.

On that fateful June day, I assumed the mantle of the 'Guardian,' the lead Sherpa climber tasked with regulating time and pacing—an invaluable role on Everest, where these factors can determine the fine line between life and death. Scaling the heights too swiftly consumes our clients' energy, leaving them vulnerable to the biting cold and exhaustion. Ascend too leisurely, and the window of favourable weather conditions, essential for summiting, slips away. Sherpas transform into meteorologists, technicians, and medics, adapting to whatever role is required for the expedition's success. When threats loom over the well-being of the ascent, a Sherpa's resolve can transmute into an unyielding determination that leaves no room for compromise. This amalgamation of roles and attributes defines the essence of a Sherpa.

The day held an added layer of significance for me beyond the ordinary. Every day, I embrace the gift of life, but this day, in particular, carried a sense of profound uniqueness. It marked my inaugural attempt at summiting Everest.

Mount Everest, that formidable colossus, loomed majestically before me —a realm of breathtaking vistas and hazardous terrain. At an imposing height exceeding 29,000 feet, it towered as the world's paramount peak. Its summit, nearly on par with the cruising altitude of commercial airliners, posed an insurmountable challenge to even the most intrepid of explorers. There, on its precipice, I stood, humbled and trembling with trepidation.

At that moment, I recalled the words of my brother—the parched throat, the ceaseless cough, the relentless battle for breath, an ordeal that even a Sherpa could not escape. At these altitudes, the body and mind push themselves to the limit, an experience amplified for foreigners attempting this perilous ascent. And then, stark reality reasserted itself —the ambition to conquer this icy and rocky titan, to momentarily discard one's oxygen mask as a testament to superhuman prowess, cast a long shadow. The stark truth loomed—hundreds had perished along this treacherous path.

'But when I say our sport is a hazardous one, I do not mean that when we climb mountains, there is a large chance that we shall be killed, but that we are surrounded by dangers which will kill us if we let them.'

George Mallory, 1924

The precise count of bodies resting eternally on Mount Everest remains elusive, but it is believed to exceed 200. Climbers and Sherpas alike repose within the mountain's embrace—hidden in crevasses, entombed beneath avalanches of snow, or exposed on the unforgiving slopes. Some remain shrouded in obscurity, while others have unwittingly become haunting markers along the route to Everest's summit. Throughout my numerous ascents, I have, retrospectively, crossed paths at least thrice with an unknown fellow adventurer. I remain ignorant of his identity, yet his relentless pursuit of dreams remains etched in my memory. Each time I pass, I offer a silent prayer for his soul.

Among the most iconic figures on Everest's haunting tableau lies the body of Tsewang Paljor, a young Indian climber who met his fate in the infamous 1996 blizzard. For nearly two decades, Paljor, known among climbers as 'Green Boots' due to the neon footwear he wore at his demise, has rested near the summit on Everest's north side. When the snow cover is scant, climbers must step over Paljor's outstretched legs as they navigate their ascent and descent from the peak.

To mountaineers, such encounters evoke a profound melancholy inter-twined with inevitability. For outsiders, the notion of a cadaver remaining in plain sight for nearly two decades may seem unfathomable. Will these mortal remains endure perpetually, or

Is there a way to address this poignant issue? As a collective, will we ever agree that Mount Everest isn't worth the cost? As my journey unfolds in this two-part narrative, the answers will weave a story of control, peril, sorrow, and astonishment.

The Altered Perception of Everest:

Mount Everest, once an untamed realm, now bears the marks of human conquest. Since the historic ascent of Tenzing Norgay and Edmund Hillary in 1953, more than 7,000 individuals, totalling over 4,000 expe-ditions, have scaled this formidable peak. In their wake, they have left a trail of waste, human excrement, and, tragically, bodies.

The motivation for the Sherpas and others employed to facilitate Everest expeditions is unmistakable—a lucrative profession. However, motiva-tions remain complex for the rest of us, often eluding definitions even within our consciousness. Professional climbers often delineate their drive from that of the majority of clients who pay for Everest ascents—a group sometimes accused of harbouring the most mundane of ambi-tions: the desire to conquer the world's highest peak for the sake of boasting rights. 'Climbing Everest is a challenge, but the true challenge lies in conquering it and keeping the conquest a secret,' quipped one observer. Yet, few would openly concede that their Everest conquest serves as a wellspring for future boasts. Instead, Everest assumes profound significance for those who fix their gaze upon it, often articu-lated in terms of transformation, the triumph over personal demons, or as the crowning achievement on a lifelong bucket list. 'Everyone carries a unique motivation,' asserts Billi Bierling, a journalist and climber based in Kathmandu.

'One seeks to scatter the ashes of a departed loved one, another ascends in memory of their mother, and some seek to confront their inner demons. In certain instances, it may be a matter of sheer ego,' adds Elizabeth Hawley, a venerable chronicler of Himalayan expeditions.

As for professional climbers, whose ardour for mountaineering transcends the limits of Everest, psychologists have for years endeavoured to dissect their motivations. Some contend that high-risk athletes, including mountaineers, are innately drawn to the thrill of sensation. However, consider for a moment the realities of scaling a mountain like Everest—weeks spent adapting to varying altitudes, a slow and arduous ascent, and the sheer willpower required to endure relentless discomfort and exhaustion. The result is an experience far removed from the adrenaline rush often associated with thrill-seeking. As Matthew Barlow, a researcher in sports psychology, aptly notes, 'Climbing something like Everest is boring, toilsome, and about as far from an adrenaline rush as you can get.'

CHAPTER 9
A LESSON IN LIFE

The Summit Promise - An Unexpected Offering, as told by Pemba.

On the 24th of May 2013, I stood at Everest Base Camp, the epicentre of human ambition, ready to embark on a mission that would soon turn into an extraordinary story. My task was to place oxygen bottles at each designated drop zone in preparation for a group of climbers who had invested their resources and dreams in pursuing the world's highest point—the summit of Mount Everest.

What transpired on the North Ridge, high above the treacherous slopes, was a profoundly personal and emotionally charged experience. At that time, I saw myself merely as a pathfinder, guiding the way for an ordinary man striving to achieve an extraordinary feat. In my mission, I was joined by three remarkable climbing Sherpas, each possessing the strength and expertise forged through countless ascents of Everest and numerous other 8000-meter peaks. Among them were three cherished friends, comrades from previous expeditions. The expedition's weightiest decision rested on my shoulders—the critical choice of when to initiate a summit bid. This decision is never straightforward. During that season on the North side of Everest, we had only two potential summit day windows: the 23rd of May and a somewhat precarious 24th of May. Ideally, we sought a three or four-day weather window to ensure a safer climb from the North Col upwards and downwards.

Unfortunately, that season, the relentless winds showed no sign of relenting. On paper, the weather on the evening of the 22nd and 23rd seemed perfect—gentle winds and a summit temperature hovering around -27 degrees Celsius. The 24th, however, loomed ominously, with forecasted winds that would breach the summit's safety threshold, dashing our hopes.

Our journey began with the treacherous crossing of the Khumbu icefall, leading us past Camp 1 and ultimately bringing us to the sterile environs of Camp 2, nestled at an altitude of 6,096 meters. The winds began to stir as we arrived, setting the stage for an unexpected turn of events. My boss called upon me to assume the role of guide, as our original guide was ailing and needing descent. Then, one of our expedition members, whom I'll refer to as Mr R, approached me with an offer that would forever shape the course of our shared journey.

'Dear Pemba,' he began, his words laden with anticipation, 'You see this jacket I'm wearing? It's a remarkable piece, worth around USD 800.' My gaze settled on the jacket he proudly displayed—a vibrant red creation from The North Face, an emblem of quality and prestige. At that juncture, such a garment was well beyond my financial reach. Most climbers relied on clothing provided by the expedition companies, or we purchased less prestigious brands with durability in mind. Mr. R continued, 'I'll gift you this jacket if you lead me to the summit. It's yours.' His proposition hung in the air, and I accepted after contemplating it.

Owning that coveted jacket would indeed be a pleasure. Its brand, synonymous with top-tier outdoor gear, added an extra layer of allure. However, this offer did not sway my resolve to guide Mr. R to the summit with all my dedication and care. Safety, above all, remained paramount. And so, our journey continued, marked by a remarkably safe ascent, void of unexpected challenges. We reached the summit of Everest, where the obligatory photographs were taken, memories etched in the thin Himalayan air, and our descent commenced.

Back at Camp 2, Mr. R asked that I dismantle his tent, promising to meet me at Base Camp to deliver the jacket as per our agreement. I obliged, and as I carried out the task, I stumbled upon an inconspicuous pair of old socks, discarded like unwanted remnants of a forgotten past. They were worn and held an unmistakable pungent odour, under-scoring why Mr. R had chosen to part with them. So, as any responsible climber committed to environmental ethics, I placed these discarded socks in the designated trash pile, destined to be ferried away from the mountain.

Upon returning to Base Camp later that day, I had completed the disposal of trash and ensured the well-being of my fellow Sherpa friends. It was then that Mr. R and I crossed paths again. 'Did you pack up everything?' he inquired, his tone hinting urgency. 'Yes,' I assured him, 'everything has been handled.' However, his next question caught me off guard, 'Are you sure, Pemba? I want your assurance that everything was packed.' 'Yes,' I reiterated, 'everything. Just a pair of old socks I disposed of in the trash.'

What followed was beyond my expectations. His voice trembled angrily as he rebuked me, 'Pemba, you've done a terrible thing. A terrible thing.' Stunned, I tried to defuse the situation, 'Sir, they were old and unsalvageable, completely unfit for use. I can buy you a new pair to make amends.' But his anger persisted. 'No, Pemba, you don't under-stand. Those socks were special. This is unacceptable.'

Baffled by the intensity of his reaction, I made a hasty return to the disposal area, hoping to retrieve those now-infamous socks. However, by the time I reached the site, many trash bags had been piled on top, obscuring any hope of retrieval. Returning to the main camp, I informed Mr. R that the socks were irretrievable. His upset remained unabated, his disappointment palpable. 'I will leave the jacket for you in Kathmandu at the Marriott hotel,' he declared before departing in a helicopter that whisked him away from Everest's unforgiving embrace.

Upon my return to Kathmandu and subsequent visit to the Marriott, no jacket awaited me. Months passed, and I received an unexpected email from Mr R inquiring about my well-being, a gesture that surprised me given our tumultuous parting. In that message, he revealed his intention to hand over the jacket if I ever visited India, his hometown in Mumbai. The proposition perplexed me, and my response was a simple acknowledgement of his message and a wish for his happiness. That was the last communication I ever received from him.

This experience etched a valuable lesson into my soul that highlighted the unreliability of promises and the unpredictability of human behaviour. I had already resolved to ensure Mr. R's safety and a successful summit, and his offer of a jacket was a gesture I never needed. Eventually, I purchased my high-quality coat from The North Face, earned through the arduous labour of guiding climbers to their dreams.

Ultimately, my journey wasn't defined by possessions or promises but by the enduring bonds forged in the crucible of Everest and the indomitable spirit of exploration that continues to beckon us to the world's highest peaks.

CHAPTER 10
CONQUERING EVEREST

The First Ascent:

We sat together in his humble kitchen, surrounded by faded photographs and mountaineering gear that had seen better days. With his weathered but still boyish face and strong hands, Pemba carried the weight of his experiences with a quiet grace. The air buzzed with anticipation, for this was not just a recollection of events but a journey back in time – a reawakening of emotions that lay dormant in the recesses of his memory.

As we delved into the details of that first expedition, Pemba Gelje's voice gained a newfound vigour. It was as if the mere act of reliving those moments breathed life back into him, as though he was donning the mountaineer's gear once more and embarking on the arduous ascent up Everest. With each word that escaped his lips, a sense of awe and wonder enveloped the room as if the very essence of the mountain had seeped into our souls.

Pemba described the exhilaration that coursed through his veins as he took his first steps on the treacherous Khumbu Icefall, grappling with the jagged ice towers that threatened to claim his life at any moment. He vividly recalled the intense cold that pierced his bones as he pitched the first camp at 21,000 feet, the suffocating altitude that sapped his strength and stole his breath away. But the final push to the summit etched itself into the deepest recesses of his being.

Pemba felt fear and determination surging as the team crept along the treacherous knife-edge ridges, grappling through gaping crevasses. It was a dance with death, a tango with destiny that demanded every ounce of fortitude and courage they possessed. The constant threat of avalanches and unpredictable weather conditions only added to the unforgiving nature of the climb, but Pemba and his team pressed on.

And then, finally, they stood upon the summit. The air was so thin that breathing felt like an arduous task, but the panoramic view before them was nothing short of celestial. Pemba cast his gaze across the sprawling expanse of the Himalayas, mesmerised by the sheer grandeur that stretched as far as the eye could see. It was a moment when time seemed to stand still – a fleeting instant where dreams intersected with reality.

But amidst the overwhelming joy and sense of accomplishment, Pemba learned humbling lessons that transcended the summit. The mountain had taught him resilience, patience, and the power of unwavering determination. It had shown him that bravery was not the absence of fear but the ability to face it head-on. It had instilled in him a reverence for nature and an acute understanding of his insignificance in the face of such magnificent forces.

As Pemba concluded his narrative, a profound silence settled upon us, punctuated only by the rhythmic ticking of an old clock on the wall. At that moment, I realised that this was more than just a story of triumph against all odds; it was a testament to the indomitable spirit of the human soul. Pemba Gelje's first ascent of Mount Everest had left an indelible mark on him. Now, through the pages of his biography, his extraordinary journey would inspire countless others to reach for their summits, whatever they may be.

The Quest for More:

Exploring the path that led Pemba to set his sights on summiting Everest multiple times has been a remarkable journey. It became clear to me that Pemba Gelje's quest for more was not merely driven by ambition but by a profound love for the mountains and a desire to push himself further than ever before. The sacred peaks of the Himalayas not only beckoned him; they seemed to call his name, echoing through the corridors of his mind.

To conquer Everest, Pemba knew he needed to prepare physically and mentally for the daunting challenges ahead. His training regimen was rigorous and uncompromising, fueled by a commitment to pushing his body to its limits. He would embark on gruelling hikes each day, slogging through treacherous terrain and braving the unpredictable elements. His muscles strained, his lungs burned, but he persevered, knowing this was the price for his ultimate pursuit.

But physical strength alone was not enough. Pemba understood that mental fortitude would be his greatest ally on the mountain. He underwent rigorous mental training, immersing himself in visualisation exercises and meditation, preparing to face the psychological battles that awaited him. From the quiet solitude of his meditation cushion, he cultivated the resilience and mental clarity necessary to navigate the treacherous slopes of Everest.

Yet, even with the most meticulous preparation, Pemba was acutely aware of the risks involved. The mountain is a merciless mistress, capable of unleashing fury on even the most seasoned climbers. He knew every step he took towards the summit was dangerous, threatened by avalanches, crevasses, and the deadly altitude. But Pemba Gelje's quest for more was not without fear; instead, it was fueled by a profound respect for the risks and an unwavering belief in his abilities.

In my research, I found countless stories of Pemba Gelje's near-death experiences on Everest. He had narrowly escaped avalanches, traversed treacherous ridges in blinding snowstorms, and faced the biting cold that gnawed at his soul. But with every harrowing encounter, he grew stronger, wiser, and more determined to press on.

Pemba Gelje's relentless pursuit of conquering Everest multiple times embodies the spirit of adventure and the innate human desire to seek out new frontiers. It is a quest that few will ever understand but one that captivates us all. His unwavering dedication, physical and mental preparation, and willingness to embrace the risks inspire those who yearn for more out of life.

As I continue to write Pemba Gelje Sherpa's story, I cannot help but be swept away by his indomitable spirit. The quest for more is not limited to climbing mountains; it resides within each of us, urging us to push the boundaries of what we believe is possible. In Pemba Gelje's journey, I find a story of adventure and a profound lesson in the boundless power of the human spirit.

The Sherpa's Role:

My fascination with the mighty Himalayas and those who conquer its peaks has led me to embark on a journey to explore the untold stories hidden within the Sherpa community. The Sherpas, a renowned ethnic group from the highlands of Nepal, have been instrumental in shaping the history of Everest expeditions. Yet, their exceptional contributions often go unnoticed, overshadowed by the glory bestowed upon the climbers they assist.

In my research, I delved deep into the Sherpas' role, seeking to uncover the essence of their strength, resilience, and unwavering support for climbers like Pemba Gelje Sherpa. Through countless interviews and hours spent immersing myself in their world, I unravelled a tapestry of stories that vividly portray an extraordinary community.

The Sherpas, resolute and fearless, are the true heroes of Everest. They are the ones who brave the treacherous slopes year after year, paving the way for climbers to reach the summit. They carry the heavy loads, risking their lives in the process, to ensure that every essential item is delivered to the high-altitude camps. Oxygen cylinders, tents, food, and equipment all pass through their capable hands as they navigate difficult crevasses and treacherous icefalls.

Their strength is awe-inspiring, fuelled by physical endurance and an unyielding spirit deeply rooted in their cultural heritage. Born and raised amidst the towering peaks of the Himalayas, Sherpas are born mountaineers. Their bodies have adapted to high altitudes, allowing them to thrive in the rarified air that leaves others gasping for breath. But it is their mental fortitude that sets them apart. Their unwavering determination to conquer the impossible and overcome the extreme is an indomitable force that propels them forward.

Throughout my conversations with Sherpas, I became acutely aware of the camaraderie within their tight-knit community. The bond between climbers and Sherpas is of trust and mutual respect, forged through shared experiences and a deeply ingrained understanding of the mountain's dangers. Each expedition relies heavily on this symbiotic relationship, with climbers placing their lives in the hands of those who know the unforgiving terrain like the back of their calloused hands.

But more than their physical prowess and mastery of the mountains make Sherpas indispensable. Their unwavering support extends beyond the physical realm as they become mentors, motivators, and providers of emotional strength. When climbers like Pemba face the inevitable moments of doubt and despair, the Sherpas often uplift their spirits and remind them of the incredible feat they are attempting to achieve.

Pemba Gelje Sherpa, a veteran climber who has scaled Everest multiple times, speaks of his admiration for the Sherpas who have accompanied him on his journeys. He describes them as his lifeline, the backbone of his expeditions. Their presence ensures his safety and provides him with the motivation and encouragement needed to push through the gruelling challenges that lie ahead.

In shedding light on the vital role Sherpas play in Everest expeditions, I hope to uplift these unsung heroes from the shadows and give credit where credit is due. They are not merely support staff but integral climbing team members, with their unwavering dedication and selflessness propelling climbers like Pemba to reach the pinnacle of their aspirations. Their stories are told, their sacrifices acknowledged, and their contributions celebrated.

Pemba Gelje Sherpa at the summit of Everest

CHAPTER 11
THE COURAGEOUS RESCUES

A Race Against Time:

Pemba Gelje Sherpa, the subject of my biographical study, had always been known for his determination and fearlessness in the mountains. But this was different. This was a race against time – a desperate bid to save a life.

As I began to recount Pemba Gelje's heroic efforts, my mind churned with the multitude of risks he faced. The sheer unpredictability of the mountain was a constant threat, with its freezing temperatures, unpredictable storms, and treacherous terrain. Every step Pemba took could be his last, as the ground beneath him threatened to give way and plummet him into the abyss.

The thin air at the high altitude added another layer of danger, making each breath a struggle. Pemba would have to push his body to its limits, fighting against exhaustion and dwindling oxygen levels, to reach the stranded climber in time. The clock was ticking, and every passing minute brought the possibility of disaster closer.

But even with all these risks looming over him, Pemba Gelje's determination to save a life burned brightly within him. Nothing could deter him from his mission. He had seen too many lives lost on these unforgiving mountains, too many souls claimed by the relentless grasp of K2. This time, he would make a difference. He would be the beacon of hope for the stranded climber, guiding him back to safety.

With every step upward, Pemba defied the odds. His crampons dug into the ice resolutely, propelling him forward amidst the biting cold. The wind howled in protest, threatening to push him off balance, but Pemba stood firm, his focus unyielding.

Time blurred as Pemba climbed higher, his body aching and protesting against the exertion. But he ignored the pain, fuelled by a single purpose – to reach the stranded climber. Minutes turned into hours, and still, he pressed on, his mind refusing to give in to the fatigue.

And finally, against all odds, Pemba reached the ledge where the stranded climber clung to his precarious existence. The relief on the climber's face mirrored the triumph in Pemba Gelje's heart. The race against time had been won; a life had been saved.

As I concluded my recounting, my hands shook with awe and reverence. Pemba Gelje Sherpa's race against time showcased not only his physical prowess but also the incredible strength of the human spirit. He had pushed forward in the face of unfathomable risks, defying the odds to save a life. It was a testament to the human spirit's indomitable will and a reminder that sometimes, even the most treacherous mountains can be conquered.

Guardian of the Mountains:

Pemba has dedicated his life to protecting and preserving the mountains he holds in such high regard. His extensive search and rescue missions have saved the lives of countless climbers who have found themselves in dire situations. With an unparalleled understanding of the treacherous terrain and a deep-rooted commitment to the safety of others, he has become the reliable beacon of hope for those lost in the unforgiving embrace of the mountains.

One incident highlights Pemba Gelje's unwavering dedication to his role as a guardian. It was the winter of 2015 when a group of climbers set out to conquer the daunting Kanchenjunga, the third-highest mountain in the world. As the expedition progressed, a fierce storm descended, engulfing the peak in blinding snowfall and whipping winds. The climbers, disoriented and battling exhaustion, were on the brink of succumbing to the brutal elements when Pemba received the distress call.

Without hesitation, Pemba gathered his team and embarked on a treacherous journey to locate the stranded climbers. Day after day, they made their way through the treacherous terrain, battling avalanches and icy slopes, driven by an unwavering determination to save lives. Finally, after what felt like an eternity, Pemba Gelje's team discovered the struggling climbers, huddled together for warmth and desperately clinging to hope.

What followed was a gruelling and painstaking rescue operation. Armed with his vast knowledge of the mountains and indomitable spirit, Pemba led the climbers down the perilous slopes to safety. His expertise in navigating the treacherous landscape kept them from the clutches of death.

However, with each successful rescue, Pemba Gelje's burden grew heavier. The emotional toll of witnessing the devastating effects of nature and the fragility of human life chipped away at his spirit. The weight of each life he saved bore down on him, leaving an indelible mark on his soul. Nights were filled with haunting dreams, the echoes of screams and prayers lingering in his mind.

At times, Pemba found solace in the mountains themselves. The vastness and grandeur of the peaks served as a refuge, a sanctuary where he could temporarily quell the turbulent emotions within. When he stood at the summit, the wind whispering its secrets in his ears, he felt connected to something greater than himself. In those fleeting moments, he understood the delicate balance between life and death and the constant dance between triumph and tragedy.

The title of 'Guardian of the Mountains' is not one Pemba takes lightly. It is a tremendous responsibility, requiring sacrifices that few can comprehend. Through my journey of unravelling Pemba Gelje's life, I have realised that his role goes beyond rescuing climbers. He is the voice of the mountains, the protector of their secrets and the silent observer of their ever-changing moods. His commitment to the mountains and the people who venture into their realms is a testament to his unwavering dedication, and though it takes a toll on his soul, Pemba remains steadfast in his duty.

In the following chapters, I will delve deeper into Pemba Gelje's extraordinary life, exploring his experiences and encounters, shaping him into the Guardian of the Mountains. From his humble beginnings in a small Sherpa village to the harrowing rescues that tested his limits, Pemba Gelje's journey is not just a story of adventure but a testament to the indomitable human spirit.

The Power of Selflessness:

In exploring Pemba Gelje's extraordinary career, it becomes evident that selflessness is at the core of his being. From the earliest days of his mountaineering adventures, Pemba has displayed a fearless determination to put the needs of others before his own. Whether guiding inexperienced climbers through treacherous terrain or risking his safety to assist fellow mountaineers in distress, Pemba Gelje's selflessness was awe-inspiring and humbling.

One incident encapsulating Pemba Gelje's selfless nature occurred during an expedition to Mount Everest. A sudden storm came roaring in, engulfing the climbers in a blizzard that blinded them and threatened their survival. Amidst the howling winds and freezing temperatures, Pemba spotted a fellow mountaineer struggling to stay upright. Without hesitation, he reached out and lent his hand, providing the much-needed stability and support.

What is remarkable about Pemba Gelje's courage is not simply the physical assistance he offered but its profound impact on the entire climbing team. In their darkest hour, Pemba Gelje's selflessness kindled the spark of hope in the hearts of his comrades. It reminded them that they were not alone in their battle against nature's fury and that even in the face of impossible odds, acts of kindness can ignite a flame of resilience.

Through Pemba Gelje's selfless acts of bravery, we are compelled to question our motivations and actions. Are we driven solely by self-interest, or can we find our strength to put others before us? Pemba Gelje's example is a profound reminder that true courage lies in facing our fears and helping those in need.

The lessons we can learn from Pemba Gelje's selflessness extend far beyond mountaineering. In a world often characterised by individualism and self-preservation, his unwavering commitment to the well-being of others serves as a beacon of hope and inspiration. It challenges us to examine our capacity for empathy and compassion and strive for a more selfless existence.

Pemba Gelje Sherpa's story is not just about conquering mountaintops; it is about conquering our limitations and embracing the power of selflessness. His courage has reminded us of the intrinsic value of extending a helping hand and its profound impact on those we assist and humanity.

As I continue to unfold Pemba Gelje's remarkable journey, I am humbled by the depth of his character and the lessons he has taught me. The power of selflessness is a force that transcends personal gain, and Pemba Gelje Sherpa embodies this power in its purest form.

In the chapters ahead, I invite you to join me on a profoundly transformative exploration of Pemba Gelje's life and the invaluable lessons we can glean from his unwavering bravery. Together, we will venture into the heart of selflessness, unveiling the extraordinary potential within each of us to make a difference in the lives of others.

CHAPTER 12
BEYOND EVEREST

Scaling Kanchenjunga:

As a biographer and author, I have had the privilege of documenting some incredible feats in mountaineering. Stories of climbers facing treacherous conditions, conquering towering peaks, and pushing the boundaries of human endurance have always fascinated me. But when I first heard about Pemba Gelje Sherpa's extraordinary accomplishment of scaling Kanchenjunga, the world's 3rd highest peak, I knew I had stum-bled upon a story worthy of documenting.

Standing tall at 8,586 meters, Kanchenjunga has long been regarded as one of the most challenging mountains to conquer. Its formidable terrain demands the utmost skill, determination, and unwavering courage. Many mountaineers spend weeks or even months acclimatising to the harsh conditions and navigating the treacherous slopes of this majestic peak. Yet, here was Pemba, a man renowned for his exceptional mountaineering abilities, who decided to push the boundaries further by attempting to summit Kanchenjunga in just one day.

To fully comprehend the magnitude of Pemba Gelje's accomplishment, I delved into extensive research and sought out details from those who witnessed this remarkable feat. It became apparent that Pemba Gelje's preparation for this audacious endeavour was meticulous and comprehensive. He meticulously studied every inch of the mountain, planned his route, and calculated the risks. Every aspect of this venture was minutely scrutinised, leaving no room for error.

Pemba began his ascent well before dawn, navigating the steep icy slopes, treacherous crevasses, and formidable ridges with unparalleled agility. He moved with a determination that could only be described as awe-inspiring. The thin air that enveloped Kanchenjunga's summit posed an ever-present threat. Still, Pemba Gelje's unwavering resolve propelled him forward, defying the human body's limitations and the sceptics who doubted his audacity.

Throughout his journey, Pemba drew upon his years of experience and wits, making split-second decisions that could mean the difference between life and death. His unwavering focus and determination propelled him forward, defying physical exhaustion and braving bone-chilling temperatures that would freeze any ordinary individual.

As the hours ticked away, Pemba Gelje's mission seemed unlikely to succeed. Yet, in a display of sheer willpower and raw determination, he pressed on. Pemba forged ahead with an exhilaration that could only come from knowing he was on the verge of achieving the impossible. The peak, shrouded in an ethereal mist, was a testament to the countless challenges he had overcome.

And then, as the sun descended, bathing the world in golden hues, Pemba stood atop Kanchenjunga's magnificent summit. At that moment, the time it was seemed to stand still. The world held its breath, transfixed by the extraordinary triumph of this mighty Sherpa mountaineer.

Pemba Gelje's remarkable feat of scaling Kanchenjunga in a single day shattered preconceived notions of what was possible in mountaineering. He had not only conquered the mountain; he had triumphed over the limitations of the human spirit.

Through individuals like Pemba, we are reminded of the boundless potential within each of us. As I delved deeper into Pemba Gelje's story,

I couldn't help but reflect on the power of human determination, the indomitable spirit that pushes us to go beyond what seems humanly achievable.

Pemba Gelje's ascent of Kanchenjunga in a day will forever stay etched in the annals of mountaineering history as a testament to human will, resilience, and the unwavering desire to push the boundaries of what is possible. And, as I pen down these words, I am honoured to have the opportunity to share Pemba Gelje Sherpa's astonishing journey with the world and to shed light on the remarkable feats achieved by those who dare to rise above the ordinary and conquer the seemingly impossible.

Adventures in the Himalayas:

As a biographer and author, my passion lies in narrating the remarkable lives of individuals who have challenged the odds and left an indelible mark on the world. Pemba Gelje Sherpa, the subject of my current project, embodies the spirit of adventure and resilience that has captivated readers worldwide. In this chapter, I delve into the exhilarating experiences of Pemba Gelje's expeditions to Manaslu and Cho Oyu, where he faced daunting challenges and achieved extraordinary triumphs.

My research revealed that Manaslu, standing tall as the eighth-highest mountain in the world, was a formidable adversary even for the most seasoned climbers. Pemba Gelje's decision to conquer its treacherous slopes was a testament to his unwavering determination and love for the mountains. Joining a small team of skilled mountaineers, Pemba embarked on an unforgettable journey to scale the heights of this majestic Himalayan peak.

The climb began in the early hours of a chilly morning, the crisp mountain air biting at our faces, fueling our adrenaline. Each step brought us closer to the summit and the daunting challenges ahead. We navigated treacherous icefalls, crossed precarious snow bridges, and battled against fierce winds that threatened to sweep us away. Pemba Gelje's expertise and resilience were a guiding light, ensuring the team's safety even in the most precarious situations.

Days blurred into nights as we ascended higher and higher, the scenery transforming into a surreal white paradise. The daunting altitude left a relentless weight on our chests, testing our physical and mental limits. However, Pemba Gelje's stoic demeanour and contagious enthusiasm kept our spirits alive, pushing us to conquer our fears and embrace the unknown.

Finally, after weeks of enduring extreme conditions and arduous exertion, we stood in awe at the summit of Manaslu. The vista that stretched before us was breathtaking, with the surrounding peaks rising as if in applause for our triumph. It was a moment of sheer euphoria, feeling intimately connected to nature's vastness and celebrating the human spirit's victory.

Conquering Cho Oyu:

The allure of the Himalayas continued to call out to Pemba, and next on his list was the majestic Cho Oyu. Often overshadowed by Everest, this sixth-highest peak holds its unique charm and challenges. My research revealed its sheer size and formidable weather conditions made it a daunting undertaking for even the most experienced climbers. But Pemba was undeterred, ready to embrace the unknown once again.

As Pemba and his team embarked on their journey to conquer Cho Oyu, they faced many obstacles that tested their resolve. The cold winds, biting temperatures, and treacherous icefalls relentlessly attempted to halt their progress. But Pemba was not one to be easily deterred. With his unwavering focus and years of experience, he guided the team through narrow crevasses and snow-covered valleys that seemed to conspire against their success.

The expedition pushed us to our physical and mental limits, demanding unwavering determination and strength. We witnessed avalanches cascading down the slopes, a chilling reminder of the formidable forces of nature that surrounded us. Yet, amidst the challenges, we found moments of camaraderie and connection, forging an unbreakable bond that comes through shared challenges.

Finally, after weeks of battling against the elements, Pemba and his team emerged victorious, standing atop the summit of Cho Oyu. The view from the top was nothing short of extraordinary. The snow-covered peaks stretched as far as the eye could see, reminding us of the vastness and beauty of the Himalayas. It was a moment of triumph, achieving what seemed impossible and reaffirming our connection to the mountains that had tested us in ways we could not fathom.

Pemba Gelje Sherpa continues to inspire us with his unwavering determination and indomitable spirit with each expedition. Through his remarkable adventures in the Himalayas, he reminds us that we can conquer even the most formidable mountains, both within and outside ourselves, with perseverance and passion.

Conquering K2:

K2 stood before me, its towering peak piercing through the grey clouds that shrouded the mountain. I couldn't help but feel trepidation and excitement coursing through my veins as I prepared to recount Pemba Gelje Sherpa's audacious attempt to conquer this formidable giant. As a biographer and author, it was my duty to bring his story to life, to capture the essence of his courage and determination.

Pemba, a Sherpa with a heart of steel and a spirit that knew no limits, had faced numerous challenges throughout his mountaineering career. His journey to K2 was no exception. The Himalayas held a mystique and a danger, but K2 held a reputation that elevated it above all others. Known as the 'Savage Mountain,' it stood as a testament to the indomitable human spirit, defying all attempts to tame it.

Pemba, accompanied by a select team of seasoned climbers, embarked on this treacherous expedition. The air grew thin as they ascended, each step fraught with potential peril. The terrain beneath their feet shifted constantly, forcing them to navigate through narrow ridges and crevasses that threatened to swallow them whole. Avalanches cascaded down the mountain, roaring like an angry beast as if warning them of the impending danger ahead.

The cold bit through their clothing, seeping into their bones as they battled the elements. The winds howled relentlessly, clawing at their faces and snatching their breath away. Frostbite threatened to claim their fingers and toes, turning them into cold, lifeless appendages. Yet, Pemba and his team pushed forward, unfazed by their brutal conditions.

But it wasn't just the weather that posed a threat. The K2's steep slopes hid potentially deadly traps within its icy embrace. The risk of falling, of tumbling down into the abyss, hounded their every step. Every placement of their crampons had to be precise, every ice pick strike calculated. There was no room for error in this cruel game of survival.

As day turned into night, Pemba and his team huddled in their tents, seeking solace and warmth amidst the unforgiving surroundings. The silence of the mountain enveloped them, broken only by the occasional crack of ice or the distant rumble of an avalanche in the distance. Their task weighed heavily on their minds, but their resolve remained unyielding.

And then, one fateful morning, the weather relented, offering them a fleeting window of opportunity. Pemba took the lead, driven by a sense of purpose and an unbridled desire to conquer the unconquerable. His ice axe dug into the ice with a resounding thud, propelling him forward, higher and higher. The freezing wind whipped against his face, attempting to snuff out his spirit, but he pressed on.

Fatigue clawed at his body as he neared the summit, his muscles screaming in protest. Doubt threatened to seep into his mind, attempting to undermine his confidence. But Pemba refused to surrender. With each laboured breath, he summoned his strength, drawing from his determination to push forward.

And then, with the sun illuminating the cloudless sky, he reached the pinnacle of K2. The air was thin, but victory tasted so sweet. Time stood still as he soaked in the breathtaking view, the triumph painting a smile across his weary face. He had conquered the Savage Mountain, defied the odds, and etched his name into the annals of mountaineering history.

Pemba Gelje's daring ascent of K2 was a testament to human resilience and the indomitable spirit within us all. His triumph reminded us that the impossible can be made possible through unwavering determination and belief in the face of impossible odds. As I pen his story, I can't help but feel a surge of admiration for this Sherpa who dared to dream big and achieve the extraordinary.

Everest, crossing the perilous Khumbu Ice Fall.

CHAPTER 13
THE LANGUAGE OF THE MOUNTAINS

Sherpa, the Language of the Mountains:

Effective communication becomes paramount in mountaineering, where every step can be a matter of life or death. The Sherpa people have long understood this, weaving their language into the very fabric of their mountainous lives. The Sherpa language is not just a means of communication but a tool for survival, connecting individuals in practical and spiritual ways.

As I dug deeper into the Sherpa vocabulary, I discovered a rich tapestry of words that illustrated their unique relationship with the mountains. Take, for example, the term 'chomolungma,' which means the goddess of the mountains. This single word encapsulates the Sherpa's deep reverence for the Himalayas and their belief in a divine presence that watches over them on their treacherous journeys.

Similarly, the Sherpa language is replete with words describing the mountains' natural elements. Words like 'gyaljen,' meaning snow, and 'lumdhum,' meaning ice, are used to navigate the treacherous terrain. These words are not just practical tools but a testament to the Sherpa's intimate understanding of their surroundings, their ability to read the subtle signs that nature provides and their unwavering respect for the mountains that have shaped their lives.

But it is not just the vocabulary that sets the Sherpa language apart; it is the culture of communication it fosters. From a young age, Sherpa children are immersed in a world where clear and concise communication is valued. Every morsel of information, every gesture, and every word has significance. It is a culture that prizes effective communication not just as a means to an end but as a means of human connection and understanding.

In the mountains, where the stakes are high and verbal communication is often challenging due to the harsh conditions, the Sherpa language becomes a lifeline. Sherpas have honed their ability to communicate non-verbally, using intricate hand gestures, facial expressions, and even subtle changes in breathing to convey their intentions and emotions. These non-verbal cues may seem insignificant to an outsider, but to the Sherpa people, they are nuanced forms of communication that can mean the difference between life and death.

Over time, I began comprehending the profound cultural significance of communication in the mountains. The Sherpas understand that their survival depends on their ability to read each other's signals, to listen keenly to the whispers of the natural world around them, and to embody a spirit of collaboration and trust. It is a lesson extending far beyond the mountains, reminding us of the power of effective communication and the deep connections it can forge.

As I immersed myself in the Sherpa language and the broader culture, I couldn't help but be in awe of the Sherpa people's wisdom and resourcefulness. Their language, with its unique vocabulary and cultural importance, held secrets that would forever change my understanding of mountaineering and human connection. As I continued to write the biography of Pemba Gelje Sherpa, I vowed to honour their language, mountains, and extraordinary way of life.

The Multilingual Mountaineer:

Hailing from the breathtaking region of Solu-Khumbu in Nepal, Pemba Gelje's multilingualism is deeply rooted in his upbringing. Growing up in a community where multiple languages intermingled, he effortlessly assimilated Nepali, Hindi, English, and Tibetan nuances. From a young age, Pemba recognised that linguistic versatility would be invaluable for navigating the diverse international community of climbers who flock to the Himalayas.

Observing Pemba in conversation is a truly remarkable sight. His proficiency in each language is unparalleled, as he seamlessly transitions between them, adapting his tone and cadence to match the speaker he interacts with. His command over Nepali allows him to connect deeply with fellow Nepalese climbers, fostering a sense of camaraderie and trust. His fluency in Hindi bridges cultural gaps when communicating with climbers from the Indian subcontinent, forging bonds that transcend linguistic barriers.

But Pemba Gelje's mastery of English truly sets him apart on the international mountaineering stage. His eloquence in English enables him to articulate his experiences, share his vast knowledge of the mountains, and engage with climbers from all around the globe. Through his linguistic prowess, Pemba has become a cultural intermediary, adept at conveying the Himalayas' rich traditions, folklore, and history to an international audience.

Beyond his linguistic skills, Pemba Gelje's fluency in Tibetan widens his circle of connectivity even further. Tibetans have a long-standing relationship with the Himalayas, and their mountaineering expertise is renowned. Pemba Gelje's ability to converse fluently in their language earns him admiration and opens doors to valuable insights and knowledge unique to their culture. This nuanced understanding of Tibetan mountaineering traditions has been a remarkable advantage, propelling Pemba to new heights of success.

Pemba Gelje's linguistic dexterity has become a source of admiration and admiration in the global mountaineering community. His language skills have allowed him to forge meaningful connections with climbers worldwide. He is celebrated for his climbing achievements and his ability to bridge gaps, build bridges, and create a sense of unity among a diverse group of individuals bound by a shared passion for the mountains.

As I delve deeper into Pemba Gelje's linguistic journey, it becomes evident that his proficiency in multiple languages is not merely a professional advantage but an embodiment of his ethos. Pemba Gelje's ability to communicate with climbers in their native tongues demonstrates his deep respect for different cultures. It highlights his dedication to fostering mutual understanding and appreciation among mountaineers from various walks of life.

In conclusion, Pemba Gelje Sherpa's linguistic abilities have been instrumental in his mountaineering career, facilitating his interactions with climbers worldwide. His fluency in Nepali, Hindi, English, and Tibetan has allowed him to communicate effectively and connect on a deeper level, forge lasting friendships, and embrace diverse perspectives. Pemba Gelje's linguistic dexterity is a testament to his extraordinary character, portraying him as a mountaineer and a global citizen striving to create a united community of climbers that thrives on mutual admiration and respect.

Breaking Barriers Through Language:

Language, in its essence, is a key to understanding and connecting with different cultures. The ability to communicate effectively not only facilitates practical aspects of climbing but also holds the potential to create deeper connections and enrich the shared experience among climbers from diverse backgrounds. Pemba Gelje's understanding of this power has been instrumental in his ability to forge bonds with climbers worldwide, ultimately transcending any language barriers that may initially exist.

As I have immersed myself in this book's research, I have encountered numerous instances where Pemba Gelje's language proficiency has significantly influenced his mountaineering endeavours. Pemba, a fluent speaker of his native Sherpa language and Nepali and English, has repeatedly demonstrated how language can be a powerful tool in facilitating communication, enabling him to navigate complex situations in the mountains. Whether coordinating logistics with his fellow climbers or effectively interpreting complex technical instructions, Pemba Gelje's linguistic skills have allowed him to bridge any gaps that may arise due to differing cultural backgrounds.

One particularly compelling example from my research is Pemba Gelje's experience during an expedition to Mount Everest. Amid a treacherous ascent, Pemba found himself alongside a climber from France, unable to communicate verbally due to their language barrier. However, Pemba Gelje's eloquent use of body language and his ability to grasp a few key French phrases created a unique form of communication that transcended words. Through gestures, facial expressions, and an unwavering sense of trust, Pemba and his French companion could navigate the treacherous terrain, relying on a shared understanding of non-verbal cues and a mutual goal - reaching the summit.

This extraordinary incident exemplifies the profound impact that language can have on forging connections and enhancing the mountaineering experience. Pemba Gelje's ability to adapt, understand nuances, and communicate effectively enables him to overcome the barriers of language and culture effectively. In doing so, he empowers himself and fosters a sense of inclusivity and empowerment among his fellow climbers.

Pemba Gelje's belief in the power of language extends beyond practical communication, imbued in his approach to mountaineering and his desire to break down barriers. Through his extraordinary journey, Pemba has not only pushed the boundaries of what is physically possible but has also demonstrated the immense potential for language to forge connections, bridge cultural divides, and enrich the mountaineering experience for all involved.

In my continued exploration of Pemba Gelje's life and accomplishments, I am continually struck by how he embodies the transformative power of language. His story is a testament to the impact of effective and inclusive communication in mountaineering and every aspect of life. In the chapters that lie ahead, I intend to delve deeper into this aspect of Pemba Gelje's journey, uncovering the personal anecdotes, challenges, and triumphs that highlight the true power of language in breaking barriers and enhancing the human experience.

CHAPTER 14
A LIFE OF SERVICE

From Guide to Lifesaver:

When I first met Pemba Gelje Sherpa, I was captivated by his humble demeanour and twinkling eyes that reflected a lifetime of mountain adventures. His weathered face told stories of the countless treks he had embarked upon, his body a testament to the physical demands of his profession. As a biographer and author, I must unearth the intricacies of his life to reveal the layers of his character that go beyond the surface of a mere job title.

Pemba Gelje's introduction to mountaineering began in his early years when he decided to run away from the monastery where he served as a monk. With starry-eyed dreams of unravelling the mysteries hidden within the treacherous slopes, he set out on a path that would forever shape his destiny. Pemba worked under seasoned guides in those early years, absorbing their teachings enthusiastically. He honed essential skills such as navigation, survival techniques, and the profound ability to read the mountains.

For Pemba, guiding others through the Himalayas' treacherous beauty was a means of earning a living and a solemn responsibility. He understood the dire consequences of even the slightest misstep and developed an unwavering commitment to ensuring the safety of those in his care. This dedication eventually led him to forge a new path to see him rise from a guide to a high mountain rescue instructor.

The transition was a challenging one. As part of his IFMGA (International Federation of Mountain Guides Association) qualification, he spent time in Switzerland, living on a diet of bread, bananas and water, given his limited budget. Pemba endured rigorous training and gruelling physical challenges that pushed his body to its limits. He learned advanced climbing techniques, practised complex rope systems, and familiarised himself with the latest rescue equipment. But it was not just the technical aspects that elevated him to the esteemed position he holds today; it was his unwavering courage, calmness under pressure, and unwavering belief in the value of every human life.

Over the years, Pemba has saved countless lives in some of the most treacherous conditions. His ability to think quickly, assess dangerous situations, and execute carefully crafted rescue plans has been extraordinary. From valiantly scaling glaciers to reach injured climbers hanging precariously on icy ledges to orchestrating daring helicopter rescues amidst violent storms, Pemba has become a symbol of hope in the unforgiving expanse of the mountains.

But behind every life saved, an emotional burden weighs heavily on Pemba Gelje's shoulders. The piercing sound of cries for help, the harrowing sight of injured climbers, and the heart-wrenching feeling of loss when rescues are unsuccessful are indelible imprints on his soul. Yet, despite the immense personal sacrifice, Pemba remains dedicated, carrying his responsibility with a sense of purpose that few can comprehend.

As I delve into the depths of Pemba Gelje's remarkable journey, I am reminded of the indomitable human spirit and the profound impact one can have when driven by a relentless determination to make a difference. Pemba Gelje's story is a testament to the fact that the perilous and unforgiving mountains also harbour within them the capacity for compassion, bravery, and the extraordinary will to save lives. As I strive to chronicle his life's work, I am filled with a renewed sense of awe at the heights one can reach when guided by an unwavering passion for being a lifesaver.

Navigating the Treacherous Terrain:

As a biographer and author, my path has led me to unravel the extraordinary life of Pemba Gelje Sherpa. In delving deeper into his experiences, I have become captivated by the treacherous terrain he and his fellow mountaineers navigate in their pursuit of reaching Himalayan summits. One aspect that stands out is Pemba Gelje's intensive training in longline helicopter rescue, which is critical in ensuring climbers' safety amidst the unforgiving high altitudes.

To comprehend the gravity of Pemba Gelje's training, one must understand the menacing nature of the Himalayan landscape. Towering peaks, narrow ridges, and unpredictable weather patterns converge to create an environment that demands relentless preparation and unwavering focus. Pemba Gelje's training regimen encompasses numerous facets, each designed to equip him with the skills necessary to conduct rescues in these seemingly impossible situations.

First and foremost, Pemba Gelje's training encompasses mastering the intricacies of longline helicopter rescue. Using a longline, a thick nylon rope suspended from a helicopter enables Pemba and his team to extract climbers from treacherous spots and transport them safely. Balancing himself on the edge of helicopters, Pemba must maintain complete control over the long line and ensure the climber's safety during the delicate lifting and lowering process.

Beyond mastering the longline technique, Pemba undergoes extensive training in high-altitude rescue scenarios. In these situations, every second hangs precariously in the balance, and the margin for error is tiny. Pemba Gelje's training includes simulating dangerous conditions at high altitudes, exposing him to the debilitating effects of reduced oxygen levels and extreme weather conditions. These simulations test his physical endurance and hone his mental acuity, training him to remain calm and composed in adversity.

Additionally, Pemba receives specialised training in identifying and responding to altitude-related illnesses. Acute mountain sickness, high-altitude cerebral oedema, and high-altitude pulmonary oedema are just a few of the life-threatening conditions climbers may face. Pemba Gelje's comprehensive knowledge of these ailments allows him to swiftly provide appropriate medical care, often making the difference between life and death in the unforgiving Himalayan peaks.

Lastly, Pemba Gelje's training extends beyond technical skills. An innate understanding of the mountain environment is crucial to navigating its treacherous terrain safely. Pemba immerses himself in years of mountaineering experience, honing his intuition and cultivating a deep respect for the mountains. This connection enables him to anticipate potential dangers and make precise split-second decisions, mitigating risks and ensuring the safety of climbers.

In conclusion, Pemba Gelje Sherpa's training in longline helicopters and high-altitude rescues is a testament to his unwavering commitment to the safety of climbers in the Himalayas. From mastering the art of longline operations to enduring challenging conditions at high altitudes, Pemba Gelje's training equips him with the tools needed to navigate this treacherous terrain. His expertise and calm demeanour in the face of adversity makes Pemba an invaluable figure, ensuring the safety and survival of climbers as they conquer nature's most formidable challenges.

A Hero Amongst Heroes:

Having spent months conducting research and interviewing those who know Pemba intimately, I have discovered a man whose selflessness knows no bounds. Pemba Gelje's heroism on the treacherous Himalayan peaks is remarkable in and of itself, but his unwavering commitment to helping others truly sets him apart. Countless stories of Pemba risking his safety to save fellow climbers have come to light, leaving me in awe of his courage and compassion.

One particular incident is Pemba Gelje's selfless bravery during a fierce snowstorm on Mount Everest. As the storm intensified, a fellow climber found himself stranded and disoriented, struggling to return to camp. Without a second thought, Pemba made the courageous decision to venture out into the blizzard, risking his own life to save his comrade. Battling freezing temperatures and howling winds, Pemba persisted until he found his fellow climber, guiding him back to safety, step by treacherous step.

But Pemba Gelje's impact extends far beyond his acts of heroism. His courage and selflessness have inspired an entire community of mountaineers. He has become a beacon of hope and inspiration, demonstrating true strength in conquering the mountains and looking out for one another. Through his actions, Pemba has united climbers from across the globe, creating an unbreakable bond of shared experiences and a mutual understanding of the challenges they face.

The admiration Pemba has earned from his peers is nothing short of remarkable. To be considered a hero among individuals who have already accomplished such extraordinary feats is a true testament to his character. Countless mountaineers, renowned in their own right, have expressed deep respect and admiration for Pemba. They cite his unwavering bravery, unwavering dedication, and compassion as qualities that have set him apart as a true hero amongst heroes.

What strikes me most about Pemba is his humility. Despite the accolades and admiration he has received, he remains grounded and focused on his mission. When asked about his heroic actions, Pemba often deflects the praise, instead focusing on the importance of teamwork and camaraderie amongst climbers. This humility makes him more admirable, showing his genuine dedication to the people and the mountains he loves.

Through writing Pemba Gelje's story, I hope to shed light on the often-overlooked heroes of the mountaineering community. Pemba Gelje Sherpa is a shining example of the selflessness, bravery, and compassion that can be found amidst the icy peaks of the Himalayas. His impact on the mountaineering community will forever be remembered, and his story reminds us all that true heroism lies in the willingness to put others before oneself.

CHAPTER 15
RECOGNITIONS AND ACCOLADES

A Summiter Recognized:

It was a brisk morning in late October when Pemba received the invitation to attend the prestigious conference held in Kathmandu. Standing amidst the towering peaks of his homeland, the letter seemed almost inconceivable. Yet, there it was, an official confirmation that his lifelong mission to conquer Everest had not only been accomplished but was also deemed worthy of recognition by the country's most esteemed organisation.

As we made our way through the bustling streets of Kathmandu, Pemba Gelje's excitement was palpable. The conference held immense significance for him, not only as a personal accomplishment but also as a representation of the perseverance and courage of his fellow Sherpas. It was an opportunity to shed light on the untold stories of those who tirelessly dedicate their lives to guiding climbers through treacherous mountain terrains.

We entered the conference hall, a sprawling space with vibrant prayer flags. The atmosphere buzzed with anticipation as climbers, adventurers, and mountaineering enthusiasts nationwide gathered in support.

Pemba Gelje's eyes sparkled with pride and humility, aware of the honour bestowed upon him.

As the conference commenced, distinguished speakers took to the stage, sharing their stories of mountaineering triumphs and the indomitable spirit of the Sherpa people. They spoke of the challenging conditions, the exhilaration of reaching the summit, and the unbreakable bond forged between climbers and their guides. Each word resonated deeply within Pemba, reminding him of his physical and emotional sacrifices to earn his place among these esteemed individuals.

Finally, the moment arrived. Pemba was called to the stage to receive his recognition as an Everest Summiter. Applause thundered through the hall as he ascended the steps, his heart pounding in synchrony with the reverberating claps. The esteemed representatives of the UNIRAV organisation greeted him with warm smiles, shaking his hand and presenting him with a beautifully crafted plaque commemorating his extraordinary achievement.

Pemba Gelje's journey was validated instantly, marked by unfathomable odds and endless determination. The recognition he received was not just a symbol of his triumph but a testament to the unwavering spirit of the Sherpa community. It highlighted the importance of their invaluable contributions to mountaineering and acknowledged their crucial role in making Everest conquered.

As I stood there, witnessing the culmination of years of unwavering dedication, I couldn't help but feel a profound sense of awe. Pemba Gelje's recognition as an Everest Summiter in the UNIRAV 12th National Conference was not just a title or an accolade; it was a celebration of human resilience, a testament to the power of dreams, and a powerful tribute to the courage and strength of the Sherpa people.

From that day forward, Pemba Gelje's name would forever be etched in the annals of mountaineering history, inspiring future generations of climbers and Sherpas alike. And as his biographer and author, it was my privilege to immortalise this pivotal moment in the pages of his captivating life story.

Conquering New Heights:

Pemba Gelje's insatiable thirst for adventure and unwavering determination to succeed had already propelled him to great heights – both figuratively and literally. During the Himalayan Outdoor Festival, I witnessed firsthand the magnitude of his triumphs and the raw talent that set him apart.

One particular event, the DYNO comp, captivated the attention of both climbers and spectators alike. The DYNO comp, short for dynamic movement competition, focuses on explosive and powerful manoeuvres that require climbers to leap from one hold to another, defying gravity with their precise timing and agility. It is an exhilarating display of strength and skill, an actual test of a climber's ability to conquer new heights.

In the DYNO comp of the Himalayan Outdoor Festival, Pemba emerged as the reigning champion, leaving his competitors in awe of his talent and determination. The way he effortlessly propelled himself from one hold to another, his body moving with the grace and precision of a seasoned dancer, was a sight to behold.

What truly set Pemba apart was his ability to remain calm under pressure, trust his spontaneous movements, and push aside any doubt or fear that threatened to hold him back. As I watched him prepare for each dyno, I noticed the focused expression on his face, a steely determination that mirrored the rugged mountain peaks he had conquered.

But it wasn't just his technical prowess that impressed me. Pemba had an unwavering passion for climbing that permeated his every move. With each dyno, he seemed to defy gravity, defying the laws of nature that had confined others to the ground. It was as if he had unlocked a secret language with the rocks, a unique connection that allowed him to move seamlessly through the air.

As I delved deeper into Pemba Gelje's climbing career, it became evident that his triumph in the DYNO comp was just one of the many milestones he had achieved. From his early days as a novice climber in the rugged peaks of the Himalayas to his conquest of the world's tallest mountains, Pemba had consistently proven himself as a force to be reckoned with.

His achievements in various climbing competitions were a testament to his hard work, discipline, and relentless pursuit of greatness. But his unwavering spirit and unyielding determination truly set him apart. Pemba had conquered the physical challenges of climbing and the mental and emotional hurdles that threatened to hold him back.

As I continued to uncover the triumphant stories of Pemba Gelje Sherpa, I was struck by the resilience and indomitable spirit that defined him. His journey to conquer new heights was an inspiring story of human perseverance, a reminder that no obstacle was insurmountable if one dared passionately chase one's dreams.

With each competition he won, Pemba left an indelible mark on climbing. His first-place victory in the DYNO comp during the Himalayan Outdoor Festival was just the beginning of a remarkable saga. This story would inspire climbers for generations to come.

In the end, Pemba Gelje's triumphs were not simply about conquering new heights physically. They were a manifestation of his unyielding spirit, his refusal to be confined by the world's limitations. Through his passion for climbing, Pemba had become a symbol of human potential, a testament to the extraordinary heights that can be reached when one dares to dream and relentlessly pursues their passion. And his saga was only beginning.

Appreciation and Admiration:

Pemba didn't just stumble into the world of climbing; he embraced it with an enthusiasm that was evident to all who had the privilege of witnessing his ascent through the ranks. His route-setting skills were unrivalled, and he had an innate knack for creating challenging and exhilarating climbing routes that pushed participants to their limits. This ability garnered him the recognition and appreciation he rightly deserved.

The first time I met Pemba, his passion for climbing was palpable. There was an undeniable fire in his eyes as he spoke about the sport he loved, and it was contagious. His magnetic personality drew people to him, and his enthusiasm was infectious. It was no surprise then that his contributions to the climbing community were met with such overwhelming appreciation.

National and international competitions became the stage where Pemba Gelje's talents truly shone. Time and time again, he proved his mettle, securing second place in national competitions and solidifying his reputation as a force to be reckoned with. It was a testament to his dedication, skill, and unyielding determination.

But not just the accolades and podium finishes earned Pemba the admiration of his peers. It was his unwavering commitment to safety and ethics in climbing that truly set him apart. He was vocal about the importance of responsible climbing practices, advocating for Leave No Trace principles and conservation efforts. Pemba understood that the mountains were not just a playground for climbers but fragile ecosystems that needed to be respected and protected. His advocacy work and leadership were met with deep admiration, further solidifying his position as a respected figure in the climbing community.

The appreciation that Pemba received was not limited to the climbing community alone but extended to the broader public. His story and achievements captured the imagination of countless individuals who saw him as a symbol of determination and perseverance. Many were inspired by his relentless pursuit of excellence and unwavering commitment to his craft. Pemba had become a role model for aspiring climbers and outdoor enthusiasts, both young and old.

As I have delved deeper into Pemba Gelje's journey, it has become clear that his appreciation and admiration were not merely a product of his climbing prowess but a reflection of his character and his profound impact on those around him. His accomplishments were born from dedication, hard work, and an unwavering belief in himself. Pemba Gelje's story is not just about climbing; it is a testament to the human spirit and the ability of one individual to inspire and uplift others.

In recounting the appreciation Pemba has received for his route-setting skills and his impact on the climbing community, I feel privileged to be able to share this remarkable journey with the world. It is a story of passion, perseverance, and the unbreakable bond between a man and the mountains. Through his achievements and the admiration he has garnered, Pemba has left an indelible mark on the climbing community and beyond, forever etching his name in the annals of mountaineering history.

CHAPTER 16
EARTHQUAKE, 2015

In the captivating narrative that follows, I delve into the heart and soul of a remarkable individual, a true exemplar of resilience and courage. This chapter, penned by none other than the subject of this biography, Pemba Gelje Sherpa, offers a unique perspective, a personal testament to the experiences, trials, and triumphs that have defined his extraordinary journey.

Wrath of the Mountain - A Fateful Afternoon:

On the 25th of April 2015, as the sun bathed the Himalayan expanse in its warm, golden embrace, the sky painted itself in a flawless shade of blue. Only the gentlest wisp of clouds dared to mar its perfection. Although thin at this lofty altitude, the air felt remarkably crisp, as if it had been freshly plucked from the lips of celestial beings. Everything seemed to align, heralding the perfect opportunity for a summit attempt —a window of hope amidst the towering challenges of Mount Everest.

But as fate would have it, the serenity of that moment was about to be shattered. Suddenly, the very ground beneath us began to quiver and shake as though a stampede of a hundred fully laden yaks bore down upon us. I lifted my gaze toward the glacier, my eyes widening in disbelief. What had once been a serene, glistening expanse had transformed into a monstrous juggernaut, a titanic wall of white, thundering toward us with terrifying velocity. It was a tidal wave of destruction, a torrent of snow, ice, and rock, a behemoth of nature's fury unleashed, hurtling at a breakneck speed, perhaps eighty feet high, or even more. It was an avalanche, an explosive force born of a cataclysmic event—a 7.8-magnitude earthquake that had struck Nepal and its neighbouring lands.

As the avalanche bore down upon Everest Base Camp, I was torn between knowing and not wanting to believe. A sense of powerlessness overcame me. The monstrous avalanche devoured the mountain and everything in its path, from the tents to the people who had been upon it. It felt like the very earth had opened up, swallowed everything whole, and closed its gaping maw, leaving only devastation and despair behind.

I felt my heart plummet within my chest. With a heavy heart, I knew the avalanche would have devoured everyone and everything that stood in its way. Two expeditions had been on the mountain, their members residing around Camp 2. My thoughts raced to the grim reality of the situation—people had most likely lost their lives. Avalanches had visited this sacred peak before, but this one, I feared, would be the most merciless of them all.

As the chaos unfolded around me, Everest Base Camp, the place I had come to know so well, was irrevocably altered. Familiar landmarks that once provided a sense of orientation were now conspicuously absent. The Norwegian trekking company, Jagged Globe, with its distinctive blue and white banner, the well-trodden trail leading to Crampon Point —gone. A nightmarish landscape of rock and ice debris lay in their place, shrouded in a dense, eerie fog that clung to the camp like a ghostly shroud. The snow began falling as if Nature wept for the horrors she had unleashed.

As I took in the surreal, post-apocalyptic scene, the memory of another tragedy struck me—just a year prior, in 2014, sixteen Sherpas had perished in the Khumbu Icefall. How could such a calamity repeat itself? Was it the mountain's way of reminding us of our fragility, of our audacity in intruding upon its sacred domain?

The devastation, post the aftershock. (Photographs courtesy of the global press)

Amidst the trembling ground and chaos, my foremost concern was the safety of our climbers at Camps 1 and 2 above. I vividly recalled my close brush with an ice avalanche in 2005. I knew the perils in the Western Cwm, the narrow glacier valley above the treacherous Khumbu Icefall. It was a stark reminder that our preconceptions about safety and risk could be woefully misguided.

The aftermath was nothing short of a grim tableau of survival and tragedy. Bodies lay strewn about, some lifeless, others clinging desperately to the remnants of their existence. Resources were scarce, and the odds impossible. Doctors worldwide, wilderness EMTs and first responders toiled relentlessly, battling against time to save lives. Ten patients were laid before Everest ER, the makeshift medical facility, each struggling to maintain their grasp on life. The dead were wrapped in torn, bright yellow tent fabric and set aside. Two of my friends and fellow guides worked tirelessly to stabilise the broken pelvis of a Japanese climber they had never met. The scene was one of relentless determination but also one of overwhelming helplessness.

Rescue, trying to find trapped climbers. (Photo by courtesy of CNBC)

In the face of such colossal devastation, I couldn't help but realise the brutal truth—there were simply too many victims to count and far too many to save, given our limited resources. Some had already succumbed to the unforgiving embrace of Everest, while others teetered on the precipice of life and death. It was a heart-wrenching choice that had to be made—focus our efforts on those who stood a chance at survival. This was the unbearable reality that we had to confront.

Amidst the chaos, I encountered a friend, his form shrouded in blood, wrapped in a sleeping bag, and seated on the icy ground. His left eye was swollen shut, and his consciousness was fleeting, marred by obvious head trauma. I helped him to his feet and led him toward one of the surviving medics for treatment.

Around us, a desperate symphony of life-saving efforts continued to play out. Doctors and responders from around the globe united in their tireless battle against the relentless toll of nature's fury. The scene persisted for hours, an unwavering testament to the resilience of the human spirit amidst unthinkable tragedy.

Days later, as the dust began to settle, I learned of the staggering toll of the disaster. The Nepalese Mountaineering Association reported nineteen deaths: ten courageous Nepalese Sherpas and five foreign climbers. Faces I had known, families I had crossed paths with—all touched by the unforgiving hand of fate. Four individuals remained unidentified, their names, nationalities, and genders forever lost to the annals of history due to the extent of their injuries. The five foreign climbers were identified as two Americans, one Chinese, one Australian, and one Japanese.

Katmandu post the 2015 earthquake. (Photographs courtesy of the global press)

For all of us who pursue the thrill of mountaineering and the allure of the world's highest peaks, we understand the inherent risks. Yet, no amount of preparation can shield us from the raw power of nature's wrath. The unpredictable Himalayan terrain is a poignant reminder that we are but visitors in a realm where nature reigns supreme. Despite accepting these inherent dangers, the magnitude of this tragedy remained incomprehensible.

In the end, this harrowing experience etched into my soul the indelible lesson that, even amidst the grandeur of the world's tallest mountains, we must never forget our vulnerability and the stark unpredictability of the natural world.

CHAPTER 17
THE MOUNTAINEER'S CODE

Respect for the Mountains:

Delving into mountaineers' deep respect for the mountains, I have understood that it is not simply a matter of conquering the summit. It goes much deeper than that. It is about the connection forged between the climber and the mountain, a bond built on mutual admiration and understanding.

Mountaineers understand the delicate balance of these incredible formations and are keenly aware of the need for responsible climbing practices. They recognise that a misplaced step or a careless action can have catastrophic consequences, not just for themselves but for the mountain itself. They comprehend the power and unpredictability of nature and approach their expeditions with caution and reverence.

In my research, I have discovered that these climbers are often deeply concerned with preserving these sacred spaces. They recognise that mountains are not just playgrounds for their adventurous pursuits but natural ecosystems supporting a delicate web of life. They understand that these pristine environments are in constant danger from climate change, pollution, and over-tourism.

Mountaineers, with their boots on the ground and hands on the rocks, advocate for responsible tourism and environmental sustainability. They recognise that their actions can have lasting effects on the mountains and the communities that call them home. They strive to leave behind only footprints and minimise their impact on these fragile ecosystems.

In their pursuit of personal triumph, these climbers have developed a remarkable appreciation for the mountains. It is not a blind ambition that drives them but a profound love and respect for these awe-inspiring creations of nature. They understand that the hills are not to be conquered but to be respected and revered.

As I delved deeper into mountaineering, I became enamoured by the passion and dedication these climbers bring to their craft. Theirs is not a quest for glory or fame but a lifelong journey to connect with the mountains and protect these sacred spaces. Their stories are not just stories of personal triumph but powerful reminders of our collective responsibility to preserve the natural wonders of our planet.

During my research, I have met many climbers who have shared their incredible experiences and insights. Their stories have enriched my understanding and ignited a flame within me to advocate for responsible climbing practices and preserving these sacred mountains.

In the chapters in this book, I will introduce you to one such moun-taineer whose remarkable journey embodies the ideals of respect for the mountains. Pemba Gelje Sherpa, a man with a deep-rooted connection to the mountains, will take us on an unforgettable expedition through the peaks and valleys of the Himalayas. Through his experiences, we will witness the importance of responsible climbing practices and the need to preserve these sacred spaces.

So, let us embark on this extraordinary journey of discovery together as we delve into the heart of mountaineering and explore the profound respect that these climbers hold for the mountains. Through these stories, we will gain a greater appreciation for these majestic formations and be inspired to become stewards of the mountains, ensuring their preservation for generations to come.

Camaraderie and Collaboration:

As a biographer and author, I have delved deep into the lives of countless individuals, capturing their triumphs, struggles, and the remarkable human spirit that propels them forward. One such individual is Pemba Gelje Sherpa, the legendary mountaineer whose stories of bravery and resilience have captivated the world.

In my research on Pemba and his incredible journey, I couldn't help but notice a recurring theme - the undeniable camaraderie and collaboration that exists within the mountaineering community. It is a bond that goes beyond mere friendship, forged in the crucible of shared challenges and nurtured by a profound understanding of the risks and rewards that await them on the mountains.

Exploring this topic further, I spoke to experienced climbers and explored their experiences to uncover the essence of this unique bond. I discovered a support network built on trust and mutual respect. The network extends beyond nationalities, cultures, and individual goals. Regardless of one's background, when climbers set foot on the treacherous slopes, they become part of a close-knit family that transcends all boundaries.

While climbing mountains may appear to be an individual endeavour, the reality is far from it. Every expedition requires a cohesive team, where trust is paramount. The climbers rely on each other's skills, judgment, and, most importantly, unwavering support. In the face of adversity, they stand together as a collective force, ready to overcome Mother Nature's obstacles.

Witnessing this spirit of collaboration firsthand during my research was both humbling and awe-inspiring. The mountaineering community is built on a foundation of selflessness and a shared passion for the mountains. When one climber stumbles, others lend a helping hand, even at the cost of their dreams. This sense of interconnectedness transforms the harsh mountain landscape into a harmonious symphony of souls, each playing their part in pursuing a common goal.

Through this bond, climbers find solace in the face of danger. They draw strength from the knowledge that their fellow climbers will be there in their time of need, and they reciprocate this unwavering support. In the crucible of the mountains, friendships are forged that can withstand the harshest of trials and endure long after the expeditions have ended.

Pemba Gelje Sherpa, the epitome of resilience and perseverance, embodies these principles of camaraderie and collaboration. Throughout his illustrious career, Pemba has scaled the highest peaks and mentored and inspired younger climbers, passing on his wisdom and experience. He understands that the spirit of collaboration is vital for success and the preservation of the mountaineering ethos.

As I delve further into Pemba Gelje's story, I am reminded of the extraordinary relationships that develop amidst the mountain world's sublime beauty and unforgiving challenges. These relationships define mountaineering as more than just a recreational pursuit but a way of life, a brotherhood and sisterhood forged in ice and stone.

In the following chapters, I will delve deeper into the lives of those who have climbed alongside Pemba, examining the intricacies of their relationships and the impact it has had on their mountaineering journeys. Together, we will unravel the stories of camaraderie, collaboration, and the unbreakable bonds that continue to shape the mountaineering community.

Leaving No Trace:

Mountaineering, by its very nature, is an audacious passion that takes climbers to breathtaking heights and unforgiving terrains. Yet, the mountaineers' respect for nature and their kindred spirit with the mountains caught my attention. They understand that their journeys must not leave lasting scars on the landscapes they traverse. Instead, they strive to honour the magnificence of their surroundings, seeking to protect and preserve the mountains for future generations.

To achieve this, mountaineers adhere meticulously to the principles of leaving no trace. Their code of ethics requires them to minimise their impact on the environment, respecting the delicate balance that exists in these remote wildernesses. Each step a mountaineer takes is carefully considered, and they strive to disturb the natural order as little as possible.

One key aspect of this commitment is waste management. Mountaineers understand the threat that human waste poses to these fragile ecosystems. Proper disposal methods are employed, ensuring that nothing is left behind. Waste is carried down the mountains and disposed of responsibly, with climbers going to great lengths to ensure no trace remains.

Furthermore, mountaineers take their role as guardians of the environment seriously, working proactively to protect the mountains they deeply love. They collaborate with local communities and organisations, engaging in initiatives aimed at conservation and sustainability. They devote their time and energy to educating others on the importance of preserving these natural wonders, fostering a sense of environmental consciousness among fellow climbers and visitors.

The efforts made to protect the fragile ecosystems of the mountains are not without challenges. Mountaineers must constantly battle against illegal logging, mining, and other harmful practices that threaten the very existence of these pristine landscapes. They advocate tirelessly for implementing stringent regulations and conservation measures, supporting the mountains and the ecosystems that rely on them.

In my quest to capture the essence of Pemba Gelje Sherpa's life, it is impossible to overlook the remarkable individuals who share his passion for leaving no trace. Their dedication to the ethics of mountaineering highlights the environmental consciousness ingrained in the mountaineering community. It is a consciousness that echoes through the valleys and peaks, inspiring those who venture into the mountains to tread carefully and treat nature with the utmost respect.

The mountains have witnessed the footsteps of countless mountaineers, yet their commitment to leaving no trace ensures that their impact is fleeting. This profound understanding threaded through the stories of Pemba and his fellow climbers, has left an indelible mark on my understanding of the delicate relationship between humans and nature. It is a lesson I will carry with me as I continue to document the extraordinary life of Pemba Gelje Sherpa, a man who embodies the spirit of the mountains and the unwavering resolve to protect them.

CHAPTER 18
LESSONS FROM
THE SUMMITS

Perseverance and Determination:

Pemba Gelje's life as a Sherpa, a member of an ethnic group renowned for their mountaineering prowess, has always revolved around the pursuit of mountaintops. From an early age, Pemba possessed an indomitable spirit and a relentless drive to conquer his limitations. He understood that success in the mountains required physical strength, mental tenacity, and an unwavering determination to push through even the most arduous circumstances.

One particular anecdote from Pemba Gelje's ascent of Mount Everest vividly demonstrates his perseverance and determination. During his second attempt, a fierce blizzard struck just as he and his expedition team reached the infamous Death Zone, the altitude where the human body's deterioration becomes inevitable. Most climbers would have turned back, recognising the danger that lurked ahead. But not Pemba. He dug deep within himself, drawing on an inner strength that seemed superhuman. Despite the blinding snow and bone-chilling cold, Pemba pressed on, inch by torturous inch, refusing to let the mountain defeat him.

Through experiences like Pemba Gelje's, we come to understand the immense importance of perseverance and determination in the face of challenges. Life often presents circumstances that test our resolve, tempting us to relinquish our dreams and aspirations. But during these moments of adversity, we must summon our inner Pemba, the unwavering spirit that propels us forward despite the obstacles that stand in our way.

While Pemba Gelje's expeditions may seem far removed from our day-to-day realities, the lessons we can learn from his journey are universal. Perseverance and determination are not innate traits exclusive to a select few. Instead, they are skills that can be nurtured and cultivated in our lives. Just as Pemba spent years preparing physically and mentally for his climbs, so can we invest time and effort in building our resilience.

One avenue for developing perseverance and determination is by setting meaningful goals. Pemba Gelje's desire to summit Mount Everest remained a constant driving force throughout his life. Similarly, identifying our aspirations and creating a roadmap for achieving them can motivate us to overcome obstacles along the way. By breaking our goals into smaller, manageable tasks, we make a structure that allows us to persevere, even when faced with setbacks and setbacks.

Another crucial aspect in fostering perseverance and determination is maintaining a positive mindset. Pemba, despite the countless hardships he faced, always carried an unwavering belief in his abilities. Like life's challenges, he understood that the mountains could be conquered with the right attitude. By cultivating a positive outlook, we gain resilience and attract the support and encouragement of those around us, creating a network of allies who bolster our determination.

Pemba Gelje Sherpa's life is a testament to the power of perseverance and determination. His unwavering spirit in the face of myriad challenges serves as an inspiration to us all. Drawing on his experiences, we are reminded that these qualities can be cultivated within ourselves. By setting meaningful goals, maintaining a positive mindset, and refusing to surrender in the face of adversity, we, too, can scale our summits and achieve greatness.

Trusting Your Instincts:

Mountaineering, with its treacherous terrain, unpredictable weather conditions, and sheer inaccessibility, demands unparalleled trust in one's instincts. Every step taken on a mountainside is a meticulously calculated risk, and relying solely on logic and analysis is insufficient. Pemba Gelje Sherpa understood this truth better than anyone. From the early days of his climbing career, he honed his innate sense of intuition, allowing it to guide him through the vast expanses of the Himalayas, where danger lurks at every turn.

For Pemba, trusting his instincts was not just a matter of life and death but a way of life. The mountains became his training ground, classroom, and laboratory, where he explored the depths of his intuition while pushing the boundaries of human capability. He learned to decipher the subtle whispers of the wind, the shifting patterns of clouds, and the slightest changes in temperature as reliable sources of information. As he ascended to dizzying heights, his intuition became his greatest ally, whispering caution when danger loomed and urging him onward when success beckoned.

But this connection between intuition and mountaineering extends far beyond the remote mountains of the world. It is a powerful lesson that can be applied to decision-making in all areas of life. How often have we found ourselves at a crossroads between logic and gut feeling? Pemba Gelje's story serves as a guiding light in those moments, reminding us to listen to that inner voice, however faint it may be. It is a voice honed by countless experiences, shaped by triumphs and failures, and attuned to the intricacies of our journeys.

Trusting our instincts requires courage, which means stepping away from the comfort of certainty and embracing ambiguity. It involves embracing the unknown, with all its potential risks and rewards. Pemba Gelje's journey is a testament to the remarkable strength within us all, waiting to be unlocked by trust in oneself.

Whether we find ourselves on a daunting mountainside or facing the complexities of everyday life, the importance of trusting our instincts cannot be overstated. It is in these moments that our intuition becomes our compass, pointing us in the direction of our true selves. The path may be treacherous, the journey uncertain, but by placing our faith in the silent whispers of intuition, we can navigate the challenges that lie ahead with clarity and purpose.

Pemba Gelje Sherpa's story is a captivating exploration of intuition's role in mountaineering and decision-making. Through his remarkable life, we discover the transformative power of trust in oneself and the endless possibilities that can be unlocked when we dare to heed the wisdom of our instincts. As I delve deeper into Pemba Gelje's extraordinary existence, I am reminded of the ever-relevant truth that trusting our instincts is a lesson to be learned and a call to action in every aspect of our lives.

Embracing the Unknown:

I have always been captivated by the stories of those who dare to venture into the unknown. The allure of the unexplored, the excitement of stepping into uncharted territories, and the beauty of embracing uncertainty have always fascinated me. In these narratives, we find the essence of human curiosity, resilience, and the relentless pursuit of growth.

In my research, I have discovered countless stories of individuals who have chosen to veer off the well-trodden path, seeking adventure and enlightenment in the vast abyss of the unknown. One such story that has deeply intrigued me is that of Pemba Gelje Sherpa, a man whose courage and determination have taken him to some of the world's most challenging and remote corners.

Pemba Gelje's journey began in the rugged mountains of Nepal, where he was born and raised. The Sherpa community, known for their mountaineering expertise and unyielding spirit, instilled in Pemba a deep love for the mountains and an insatiable thirst for exploration. From a young age, he dreamt of conquering the highest peaks and discovering the hidden treasures that lay beyond.

But what truly sets Pemba apart is his ability to embrace the uncertainties of venturing into the unknown. Rather than being deterred by the risks and dangers ahead, he thrives on the adrenaline rush accompanying each step taken into uncharted territories. Through this mindset – the willingness to embrace uncertainty – Pemba has been able to accomplish feats that most would consider impossible.

Pemba has encountered countless physical and mental challenges throughout his expeditions. He has faced them all head-on, from treacherous terrains and unpredictable weather to self-doubt and fear. And each time, he has emerged stronger, wiser, and more attuned to the power of embracing the unknown.

The beauty of stepping outside our comfort zones lies in the profound lessons that can be learned along the way. In moments of uncertainty, we discover our true potential, pushing past our perceived limitations and reaching new heights. Pemba Gelje's journey has taught me that the unknown is not something to be feared but rather a space where growth and transformation thrive.

When we embrace uncertainty, we liberate ourselves from the constraints of familiarity and open ourselves up to a world of infinite possibilities. In these moments, we truly discover who we are, what we are capable of, and what lies beyond the boundaries of our imagination.

As Pemba continues to venture into uncharted territories, he challenges himself physically and invites us to explore the depths of our fears and limitations. Through his courage and determination, he inspires us to embrace the unknown in our lives, step outside our comfort zones, and embark on our own odyssey.

In the next chapter, I will delve deeper into the lessons that can be learned from embracing uncertainty and how Pemba Gelje's journey inspires us all. We will unravel the hidden treasures within the unknown and discover our untapped potential.

CHAPTER 19
THE MAGIC
OF THE HIMALAYAS

A Journey to the Sacred:

The Himalayas, with their jagged peaks shrouded in swirling mists, have long been revered as the abode of gods. This mountain range stretches across several countries, serving as a physical and spiritual boundary between the mundane and the celestial. To understand the significance of Pemba Gelje's pilgrimage, it is essential to grasp the spiritual essence of these majestic peaks. The Himalayas are believed to be the dwelling place of Hindu gods and goddesses, with each mountain peak symbolising a divine deity. Mount Kailash, the zenith of Pemba Gelje's journey, is considered the sacred abode of Lord Shiva, the destroyer and rejuvenator of the universe.

For centuries, pilgrims have flocked to the Himalayas, seeking solace, enlightenment, and a connection with the metaphysical. These ancient traditions and beliefs, steeped in myth and folklore, hold a profound allure. As a biographer, my task is to unravel the layers of history and delve into the sacred rituals and practices passed down through generations. From the mysterious cave monasteries of Tibet to the awe-inspiring temples nestled amidst the vast expanse of the Himalayan foothills, the spiritual tapestry of this region is diverse and rich.

Pemba Gelje's pilgrimage is a microcosm of this spiritual tapestry. His journey takes him through remote villages, where he encounters wise sages and seasoned pilgrims, each with their stories of devotion and enlightenment. As he traverses treacherous terrain and battles the elements, Pemba Gelje's physical trials mirror the spiritual challenges pilgrims face throughout history. Through these trials, he discovers his strength and resolve, forging a deeper connection with the ancient traditions he seeks to uphold.

The transformative power of pilgrimage lies in traversing the mountains and the inner exploration it necessitates. The Himalayas are a mirror, reflecting the depths of one's soul and forcing introspection. Pemba Gelje's pilgrimage becomes an introspective journey, shedding layers of ego and external attachments to reveal the true self. In immersing himself fully in the rituals and practices of the Himalayan traditions, Pemba undergoes a spiritual metamorphosis, emerging from the mountains as a changed man.

In '*Step by Step*', I invite readers to embark on this spiritual odyssey, to experience the majesty of the Himalayas and the profound power of pilgrimage. Through meticulous research and immersive story-telling, I aim to transport readers to the ancient lands where gods and mortals converge, where belief and faith intertwine. I aim to reveal the timeless wisdom within these mountains, offering readers a glimpse into a realm beyond the physical, a journey to the sacred.

The Dance of Light and Shadow:

As a biographer and author, I have been fortunate enough to witness this dance many times. Through my research and interviews with climbers and mountaineers, I understood the profound impact of the play of light and shadow on their lives. It was a dance with a unique power, captivating those who dared to venture into the highest peaks.

The ever-changing interplay of light on the Himalayan peaks painted a vivid picture that mesmerised climbers and drew them closer to the ethereal beauty that lay before them. The rising sun transformed the icy landscape, illuminating the mountains with an almost blinding brilliance. The pure white snow shimmered as the light danced upon its surface, creating a mesmerising spectacle that seemed to defy the limits of nature.

But it wasn't just the physical beauty that captivated climbers. They felt a deeper, more spiritual connection with the mountains. The Himalayas, with their towering peaks reaching towards the heavens, off ered an unparalleled opportunity for transcendence. Amid the dance of light and shadow, climbers could experience a profound sense of peace and awe that few other places on Earth could provide.

For the climbers, it wasn't just about conquering the mountains. It was about becoming part of the dance itself, surrendering to the whims of nature and allowing the hills to transform their very being. They spoke of moments when time seemed to stand still, when the boundaries between earth and sky blurred, and they became one with the ethereal beauty surrounding them.

My research led me to countless stories of climbers who had experienced these transcendent moments. They spoke of the peaceful silence that enveloped them as they stood on the summit, the sheer magnitude of the mountains humbling them into silent reverence. They described the feeling of being suspended between earth and sky, their bodies infused with a sense of weightlessness and freedom.

But it wasn't just the physical sensations that were transformative. Climbers spoke of a deep connection with the mountains, themselves, and the world around them. In the dance of light and shadow, they found a mirror that reflected their own inner struggles and triumphs. The unforgiving terrain served as a metaphor for their challenges, pushing them to their limits and forcing them to confront their fears and weaknesses.

As I delved deeper into these climbers' stories, I realised that the dance of light and shadow was more than just a visual spectacle. It was a journey of self-discovery, a pilgrimage to the depths of the human spirit. It was a reminder of our own impermanence, of the ever-changing nature of life itself. And it was in this dance, in the fleeting moments of beauty and transcendence, that climbers found a profound sense of purpose and fulfilment.

The dance of light and shadow on the Himalayan peaks was a symphony of the senses, a tapestry woven by nature. It was a dance that captivated climbers, drawing them into a world where time stood still, and ordinary concerns faded into insignificance. It was a dance that offered moments of profound connection and transformation, reminding us of the beauty and wonder that can be found in even the most hostile environments.

In the pages of this book, I want to capture the essence of this dance, to paint a vivid picture of the ever-changing play of light and shadow on the Himalayan peaks and the transcendent experiences they offer. Through the stories of climbers and the exploration of the deep connection they forge with the mountains, I aim to transport you into a world where ordinary boundaries cease to exist, and the dance of light and shadow becomes a metaphor for the human spirit's infinite capacity to soar.

The Mountains Within:

Pemba Gelje's story intrigued me from the start. Born and raised in the heart of the Himalayas, he grew up surrounded by the mystic beauty and imposing might of the mountains. From an early age, Pemba felt a deep calling, a magnetic pull drawing him towards the peaks that loomed in the distance. It was as if the mountains had a secret language resonating within him.

As I sat across from Pemba, hearing the cadence of his voice telling stories of his numerous expeditions, it became clear that the mountains were not just a backdrop in his life; they were an integral part of his very being. Pemba spoke of his immense challenges on the treacherous slopes, battling against the elements and pushing his physical and mental limits. But it was not merely conquering these external obstacles that fascinated him; it was the journey within.

Pemba described how, with each step he took towards the summit, he was also ascending more, plunging into the corridors of his own soul. The solitude of the Himalayas provided him with the necessary introspective space to confront his innermost fears and doubts. Here, in the company of silence and solitude, he discovered his potential and learned to tame the raging storms that brewed within him.

The metaphorical mountains within ourselves are often more formidable than the physical ones outside. They represent the barriers we must overcome, the fears and self-doubt that hold us back from reaching our true potential. Pemba understood this better than most. Through his journeys in the Himalayas, he learned that the key to conquering these internal peaks lay in self-awareness and self-mastery.

In delving into self-discovery, I couldn't help but reflect on my journey. Like Pemba, I have faced my fair share of mountains within. As a writer, there are times when the blank page before me feels as impossible as any Himalayan peak. Doubts whisper in my ear, questioning my abilities and tempting me to give up. But I have learned from Pemba Gelje's wisdom that the only way to overcome these internal mountains is to stand tall and take that first step.

Exploring the metaphorical mountains within ourselves requires us to be brave enough to confront the hidden parts of our psyche that we would rather avoid. It demands self-reflection and self-discipline, traits that Pemba has honed through mountaineering. But it is through this journey that we find true wisdom and discover the depths of our strength.

With their awe-inspiring beauty and treacherous terrain, the Himalayas serve as a canvas for exploring the physical and internal landscapes. Pemba Gelje Sherpa's experiences in the mountains offer a profound insight into the transformative power of solitude and introspection. His story serves as a guiding light for those seeking to conquer their mountains within and unearth the hidden treasures that lie beneath the surface.

As I continue to draft the chapters of 'Step by Step,' I am reminded of the words Pemba once told me: 'The real journey, the most challenging one, lies within. It is the journey towards self-discovery and self-mastery. It is a path of confronting our deepest fears and embracing our true potential.' With these words echoing in my mind, I embark on my journey of writing this book, hoping that it will serve as a guide for others who seek to conquer their mountains within.

CHAPTER 20
THE LEGACY CONTINUES

Passing the Torch:

Throughout my research on Pemba Gelje Sherpa, I have encountered numerous instances where he generously shared his vast mountaineering experience with aspiring climbers. The joy he finds in mentoring young individuals is not to be taken lightly; a genuine passion radiates from him whenever he speaks about his role as a mentor. Witnessing his enthusiasm as he imparts knowledge and life lessons to those eager to follow in his footsteps, I am struck by his profound impact on these budding climbers.

Pemba Gelje's commitment to mentorship goes beyond teaching technical skills; it fosters a deep respect for the mountains and emphasises the importance of safety and responsible mountaineering practices. His lessons come in various forms, sharing anecdotes of triumph and peril, imparting wisdom about reading the mountains and weather patterns, and instilling within his mentees a sense of humility and gratitude for the privilege of venturing into these sacred landscapes.

The significance of Pemba passing on the mountaineering legacy cannot be underestimated. As the torchbearer of Sherpa mountaineering, he recognises the responsibility that comes with his expertise. He understands the weight of preserving and honouring the traditions and knowledge passed down through generations. Pemba sees himself as a custodian of the mountaineering legacy, ensuring that it remains alive and relevant in the face of rapidly changing landscapes and climbing practices.

Beyond the practicalities of mountaineering, Pemba believes in empowering the next generation of climbers to embrace the spirit of adventure and exploration while fostering a deep connection to nature. He understands that climbing, more than just conquering summits, is a transformative journey of self-discovery. Pemba Gelje's mentoring goes beyond imparting technical skills; he encourages his mentees to develop mental grit, resilience, and a profound appreciation for the mountains' grandeur.

In his eyes, passing the torch is not merely about transferring knowledge and skills—it is about instilling a love and respect for the mountains, nurturing an unwavering commitment to environmental stewardship, and fostering a sense of unity within the climbing community. Pemba believes that by mentoring young climbers, he perpetuates the values that have been the bedrock of mountaineering for centuries, ensuring that future generations continue to explore and protect these ethereal landscapes.

As I delve deeper into Pemba Gelje Sherpa's life and his impact as a mentor, I am captivated by his unwavering dedication to sharing his knowledge and experiences. His commitment to passing on the mountaineering legacy preserves an invaluable heritage and lays the foundation for a new generation of climbers. Pemba Gelje's selflessness and genuine joy in mentoring encapsulate the essence of being a true mountaineer.

Preserving the Mountains:

Exploring Pemba Gelje's efforts in conservation has been an eye-opening experience. From a young age, he was enamoured by the majestic beauty of the mountains and the fragile ecosystems they house. Growing up in a small Sherpa village in the heart of the Himalayas, Pemba witnessed firsthand the devastating impact of human activity on the environment. Rivers that once teemed with life now ran dry, and the once-imposing glaciers began to recede at an alarming rate. These observations spurred Pemba into action, igniting a fire within him to safeguard these natural wonders.

Pemba Gelje's commitment to preserving the mountains is unwavering. He understands that these towering peaks hold more than just physical beauty. They are sacred spaces, serving as a source of spiritual and cultural significance for communities worldwide. Pemba has dedicated himself to spreading awareness about maintaining the delicate balance between human interaction and preserving these sacred spaces.

However, Pemba Gelje's journey has been challenging. As he embarked on his mission, he encountered resistance from those who saw the mountains solely as a source of economic gain. Large-scale commercial enterprises, such as mining and tourism, threatened the very essence of these pristine landscapes, disregarding the long-term consequences for short-term profits. Pemba faced opposition and scepticism but remained relentless in his pursuit of conservation.

One particular obstacle that Pemba confronted was the need for wide-spread education about environmental sustainability. He understood that to effect lasting change; he needed to empower local communities with knowledge about the fragility of their surroundings and the importance of preserving them. Pemba initiated outreach programs, organising workshops and seminars to educate villagers, tourists, and even government officials about their vital role in protecting the mountains. By fostering a sense of responsibility and instilling a deep love and appreciation for nature, Pemba hoped to create a cohesive movement that would endure for generations to come.

I have been amazed by Pemba Gelje's tenacity and resilience throughout his conservation efforts. Despite his formidable challenges, he continues to forge ahead, undeterred by setbacks and obstacles. Through his unwavering dedication, Pemba Gelje Sherpa has inspired countless individuals to join him in the fight to preserve the mountains. His tireless advocacy has raised awareness and catalysed change in policies and practices that threaten the very existence of these natural wonders.

In conclusion, Pemba Gelje Sherpa's commitment to preserving the mountains is a shining example of what can be achieved through passion and perseverance. His tireless conservation and environmental stewardship efforts have protected the physical beauty of these natural landscapes and safeguarded the cultural heritage and spiritual sanctity they embody. Pemba Gelje's journey is a testament to the power of one individual's determination to make a difference, and his legacy will undoubtedly inspire future generations to carry on his invaluable work.

A Legacy of Inspiration:

Pemba Gelje's life has been filled with determination, bravery, and an unwavering commitment to the mountains. From his humble beginnings growing up in the remote village of Kharikhola in the Solu-Khumbu region of Nepal, Pemba Gelje's connection to the Himalayas was forged early. His seasoned mountaineer brother instilled in Pemba a deep respect for the mountains and a passion for climbing that would shape his life.

Pemba Gelje's story truly began to unfold on the jagged slopes of Mount Everest. With a spirit of adventure burning, he set out to conquer the world's highest peak. But it was not just the physical challenge of the climb that motivated Pemba; it was the opportunity to inspire others to push beyond their limits and reach for their dreams. Throughout his ascent, Pemba documented his journey through captivating photographs and poignant words, sharing his triumphs and struggles with climbers and enthusiasts worldwide.

Pemba Gelje's courageous spirit and unwavering determination did not go unnoticed. His journey resonated deeply with climbers of all backgrounds, inspiring them to pursue their mountaineering aspirations. The impact of his story rippled through the mountaineering community, spreading a sense of optimism and a belief that nothing is impossible if we are willing to persevere.

But Pemba Gelje's legacy goes far beyond the mountains. His commitment to giving back to his community and supporting young climbers from underprivileged backgrounds has left an indelible mark on the lives of countless individuals. By establishing the Pemba Gelje Sherpa Foundation, he has created opportunities for aspiring climbers to follow in his footsteps, regardless of socioeconomic status. Pemba firmly believes that the mountains should be accessible to all, and his foundation strives to remove barriers to entry, providing training, equipment, and mentorship to those who may not have the means to pursue their dreams.

As I reflect on the lasting inspiration that Pemba has provided to climbers around the world, I am struck by the profound impact of his journey. His story is not just one of personal triumph but a testament to the enduring human spirit and the power of perseverance. Pemba Gelje's legacy reminds us all that the mountains hold physical challenges and the opportunity for personal growth, self-discovery, and a profound connection to something greater than ourselves.

As I continue to unravel the intricacies of Pemba Gelje's life, I am humbled by the privilege of sharing his story with the world. Through my writing, I hope to capture the essence of his spirit, inspire others to embrace their adventures and remind us all of the lasting legacy we can leave behind when we choose to live a life guided by passion, purpose, and an unwavering belief in the power of the human spirit.

CHAPTER 21
A JOURNEY OF THE SENSES

The Symphony of Silence:

Immersing readers in the profound silence of the mountains becomes my paramount mission as a storyteller. I strive to recreate the stillness that envelops climbers, allowing them to feel the weight of each footstep, the rustle of wind through their gear, and the rhythmic beating of their hearts. Through vivid descriptions, I aim to transport readers to the awe-inspiring landscapes where Pemba flourished, to make them feel the crisp air against their skin and the tantalising taste of solitude.

The meditative quality of this sensory experience cannot be adequately described in words alone. It is a dance between the external world and the internal landscape of the climbers. In this dance, the symphony of silence becomes the conductor, guiding their thoughts and emotions through the virtuosic performance of mountaineering.

Each climber, including Pemba, becomes a soloist in this symphony, their breath becoming the rhythm that sustains them through the arduous journey. They learn to attune their senses to the subtle cues whispered by the mountains, gently coaxing them forward or urging caution. It is a constant dialogue with nature, a conversation rooted in silence.

But the symphony of silence is an external experience and an exploration of the self. In the stillness of the mountains, climbers confront their fears, doubts, and limitations. They seek solace in the vastness of the peaks, finding strength where they once felt weakness. The silence becomes a mirror that reflects their essence, transforming them in ways that words cannot capture.

Through meticulous research and interviews with those who have climbed alongside Pemba Gelje Sherpa, I have witnessed the profound impact of the symphony of silence on climbers. It is not just an absence of noise; it is a presence, a force that demands attention and respect. It is an immersion into the depths of the human spirit, where words lose meaning and silence becomes the universal language of the mountains.

In my quest to uncover the heart of Pemba Gelje's story, I have understood that the symphony of silence is not limited to mountaineering. It is a concept that resonates with all of us, regardless of our chosen paths. It is an invitation to embrace the stillness, listen to our soul's whispers, and find meaning in the spaces between the notes.

As I continue to weave Pemba Gelje's narrative, I am called to explore the symphony of silence through his remarkable experiences and within my own life. I am reminded that silence is not an emptiness to be feared but a canvas upon which the most profound truths can be painted. In silence, we truly hear the voice of our existence and find the courage to climb the mountains that lie before us. And in that silence, we discover our symphony, waiting to be heard and shared with the world.

The Colours of the Peaks:

In the foothills of the Himalayas, where time seems to stand still, I sat down with Pemba to listen to his stories of adventure and triumph. His eyes sparkled with a hint of nostalgia as he recounted the ethereal hues that danced upon the snow, the breathtaking beauty that captivated climbers from all corners of the globe.

Each morning, as the sun kissed the peaks, a delicate blush of pink would spread across the horizon, casting a rosy glow upon the towering summits. Pemba described the scene with a reverence usually reserved for sacred rituals; his voice was filled with awe and respect for the natural world. 'It was as if the mountains themselves were waking up, stretching their limbs and embracing the first light of day,' he said, his words carrying a sense of wonder.

But it was not only the morning sun that painted the peaks in vibrant colours. The ever-changing light breathed life into the mountains throughout the day, transforming them into a kaleidoscope of hues. Pemba spoke of the warm golden tones that bathed the slopes at midday when the sun stood high in the sky and cast its radiant glow upon the snow-covered peaks.

As evening approached, a cool blue descended upon the mountains as if the sky had fallen to earth. Pemba recounted the tranquillity that enveloped the landscape, the stillness that settled upon the peaks, creating a moment of serenity amid this wild and untamed wilderness. 'It was as if time stood still, and the world held its breath,' he said, his voice tinged with melancholy.

But the colours of the peaks were not confined to just the daylight hours. Pemba shared stories of moonlit nights when the mountains were bathed in silver, and the entire world seemed to glow with an other-worldly radiance. He spoke of the way the moonlight painted intricate patterns upon the snow, creating a tapestry of shadows and light that seemed to dance with every gust of wind.

As I listened to Pemba Gelje's stories, I couldn't help but be captivated by the power of his words. He had a rare ability to transport me to the heart of the Himalayas, to make me feel the crisp mountain air upon my skin and see the ever-changing colours of the peaks with my own eyes.

In writing Pemba Gelje Sherpa's story, I have endeavoured to capture the beauty of the Himalayas, to bring to life the colours of the peaks that so captivated him and countless other climbers. Through meticulous research and interviews with fellow mountaineers, I have strived to weave together a tapestry of words that does justice to the breathtaking landscapes Pemba called home.

In doing so, I honour Pemba Gelje's extraordinary achievements and the profound connection between humans and nature. For in the colours of the peaks, we find a reminder of the beauty that lies beyond our everyday lives, a reminder that the world is vast and filled with wonders waiting to be discovered.

Tasting Victory:

The moment Pemba reached the summit was like a crescendo in a symphony, a culmination of years of preparation, determination, and sacrifices. I stood in the thin air, watching sweat-slicked faces break into radiant smiles as the climbers surveyed the breathtaking landscape beneath them. A swirling concoction of emotions stirred within me, a heady mix of awe, respect, and admiration.

The summit was not just a physical peak; it symbolised the pinnacle of human perseverance and the indomitable spirit of those who dared to challenge nature's mightiest obstacle. Like an exotic spice, the taste of victory seeped into the climbers' senses, infusing every cell of their being with an electrifying energy. It was as if they had stepped into a different realm, where the air hummed with an intangible thrill.

I observed Pemba as he revelled in this moment of triumph, his eyes gleaming with joy and relief. He had faced countless obstacles on his journey, battling treacherous weather, physical exhaustion, and the constant shadow of doubt. But now, all of that seemed distant, like a faded memory. The taste of victory was tangibly present, dancing upon his taste buds, filling his lungs with refreshing vigour.

The celebration that ensued was a cacophony of laughter, cheers, and hugs. The climbers embraced each other, their grins stretching wide enough to touch the heavens. Bottles of champagne were uncorked, and the crisp bubbles mingled with the thin air, turning the atmosphere into a fizzy symphony. The mountaintop was transformed into a temple of jubilation, where fatigue melted into euphoria, and the weight of the world seemed to lift.

As I observed, I couldn't help but reflect on the significance of this moment, not just for Pemba but for all who strive to conquer their mountains. Victory, I realised, did not lie solely in conquering nature's challenges but also in the metamorphosis, it brought to the climbers. They had transformed in this overwhelming sweetness of triumph, transcending their limitations and proving the boundless depths of human potential.

In that celestial moment, surrounded by lofty peaks and jubilant climbers, I understood that tasting victory was a fleeting sensation and a nourishment for the soul. It was a reminder that dreams, no matter how colossal, were within reach if one pursued them with unrelenting perseverance. It was a testament that the human spirit, when kindled with passion and unwavering resolve, could soar to unimaginable heights.

As I pen down Pemba Gelje's incredible journey, I want to capture the physical feats he accomplished and the rich tapestry of emotions woven into his triumph. It is a story that goes beyond words, a story that demands to be savoured, and a taste of victory that lingers in the memory of climbers and readers alike.

CHAPTER 22
A LIFE OF BALANCE

Family and Mountaineering:

Pemba Gelje's love for mountaineering was unwavering, yet he understood the profound importance of family. As his biographer, I was privileged to uncover the intricate web that connected his two worlds. It was a tightrope walk, a constant negotiation between pursuing his passion for conquering the world's highest peaks and ensuring the well-being of his loved ones.

Mountaineering, by its very nature, demands rigorous training and long stretches of isolation from the comforts of home. It tests an individual physically, mentally, and emotionally. Scaling mountains' sheer danger and unpredictability can strain the most substantial relationships. Yet, somehow, Pemba managed to strike an exquisite balance between his ambitions and his family responsibilities.

Pemba Gelje's ability to maintain this delicate balance was a testament not only to his determination but also to the immense strength of the Sherpa community. Embedded in their cultural fabric was a profound respect for the power of the mountains and the need to answer its call. Even Pemba Gelje's extended family, friends, and neighbours understood the significance of his pursuits, providing a network of support that sustained him and his family during his countless adventures.

The symbiotic relationship between family and mountaineering in Pemba Gelje's life was a testament to the profound bonds that can be forged through shared aspirations. While it required immense sacrifices, it also offered immeasurable rewards. Pemba Gelje's expeditions served as instruments of personal growth for himself and his entire family, strengthening their resolve, fostering resilience, and igniting a burning passion that transcended bloodlines.

As I continued to piece together the intricate puzzle that was Pemba Gelje Sherpa, I marvelled at the steadfast support he received from his family. It painted a vivid portrait of a man who defied the odds, pushed boundaries, and understood that his dreams were his own and belonged to those who loved and believed in him.

The Inner Journey:

When I first set out to unravel the inner workings of Pemba Gelje's mind, I anticipated discovering a complex network of spiritual ideologies and practices. Surprisingly, I found a humble man with an unwavering commitment to personal growth and self-care. Pemba believes that true strength lies in the ability to remain grounded and composed amidst the chaos of life rather than seeking external validation or relying on material possessions.

One of the cornerstones of Pemba Gelje's inward journey is his daily meditation practice. Each morning, before the sun graces the mountain peaks with its warmth, Pemba retreats to a quiet corner and immerses himself in the tranquillity of his thoughts. Through mindful breathing and cultivating inner calm, he fosters a deep connection with his inner self. This deliberate practice not only helps Pemba gain clarity and focus but also serves as a source of strength during challenging times.

Maintaining balance is not limited to the realm of meditation alone. Pemba values physical fitness as an essential component of his wellbeing. Daily exercise routines help him stay strong and flexible, both physically and mentally. By nurturing his body, Pemba understands that he is promoting his mind, allowing him to tackle the arduous mountainous terrain with resilience and composure.

Pemba Gelje's journey towards self-care extends beyond his personal practices. He recognises the importance of surrounding himself with a robust support system of friends, family, and fellow Sherpas. They share in his aspirations and provide a sense of belonging and camaraderie. These relationships are a constant reminder that he is not alone in pursuing personal growth and well-being.

In navigating the demanding world of mountaineering and its pressures, Pemba also emphasises the significance of self-compassion. He acknowledges that setbacks and failures are not signs of weakness but opportunities for growth and resilience. By embracing self-compassion, Pemba becomes his own advocate, offering himself the same care and understanding he would extend to others.

In exploring Pemba Gelje Sherpa's inner journey, I realised the importance of mental and emotional well-being. The practices that Pemba has cultivated over the years serve as guideposts, offering him solace and strength in the face of adversity. From the stillness of meditation to the physicality of yoga, Pemba has unlocked the power of self-care, balancing the personal challenges of his life with utmost grace.

As I continue to delve deeper into the life and experiences of Pemba Gelje Sherpa, I am humbled by the lessons I am learning through his example. The inner journey of self-discovery and self-care is an ongoing process that requires dedication and self-reflection. It is not a destination but a continuous evolution, one that Pemba embraces fully, and in doing so, he inspires those around him to embark on their own transforming expedition.

Lessons in Balance:

One of the fundamental lessons Pemba has learned is the importance of balance. Finding equilibrium became a matter of survival in the mountains, where the tiniest misstep could lead to disastrous consequences.

Pemba honed his physical agility and mental focus, but more importantly, he learned how to balance his heart, mind, and spirit. The mountain became his teacher, guiding him towards harmony despite constant challenges.

In his pursuit of balance, Pemba found that it extended beyond his physical and mental capabilities. He started recognising the importance of equilibrium in his relationships, work, and personal aspirations. The mountains taught him that success is not measured solely by reaching the summit but rather by the journey and people accompanying us. Pemba Gelje's mountaineering achievements are remarkable, but his humility and genuine care for those around him shine through.

Pemba Gelje's quest for balance extends to his role as a Sherpa, a community leader, and a family man. Despite the demands of his climbing career, he always keeps sight of the importance of being present for his loved ones. Whether it is sharing cherished moments with his children or supporting the dreams of aspiring climbers, Pemba understands the delicate art of giving and receiving, always seeking a harmonious balance.

Beyond the physical and interpersonal, Pemba has also discovered the need for balance within oneself. The mountains have taught him the value of self-reflection and introspection. By immersing himself in the solitude of the peaks, he has learned to quiet the noise of the outside world and connect with his innermost self. This profound connection empowers him to navigate life's challenges with grace and resilience, always seeking equilibrium in adversity.

As I delve deeper into Pemba Gelje's story, I am struck by the profound wisdom he has gained through his mountaineering experiences. Lessons in balance permeate every aspect of his life, shaping him into the remarkable individual he is today. From the mountains, Pemba has learned to harmonise the various elements that make up his existence – physical, mental, emotional, and spiritual. This harmony is not a static state but a continuous, lifelong pursuit. He understands that finding balance is not a destination but a journey, and he embraces every step with unwavering determination.

Pemba Gelje Sherpa's story is a testament to the transformative power of the mountains and the lessons they teach us about ourselves and the world. Through his journey towards harmony, he inspires us to reflect on our lives and seek balance in all its forms – physical, emotional, and spiritual. As a biographer, I am truly privileged to convey Pemba Gelje's profound lessons in harmony, allowing his wisdom to touch the lives of many and inspire them to create their harmonious path.

CHAPTER 23
THE MOUNTAINS AS TEACHERS

The Art of Patience:

While exploring Pemba Gelje's life, I discovered that he possesses a remarkable virtue – the art of patience. And it is in the mountains, where time seems to have a different rhythm and the beauty of nature unfolds in all its grandeur, that this virtue truly thrives.

Climbing mountains demands a slow and steady pace, a rhythm entirely at odds with our world, where everything is fast-paced and instantaneous. Pemba understood this innate contradiction and embraced it wholeheartedly. He taught me that in the mountains, one must surrender to the pace dictated by the environment, accepting the power of patience. This art enables a climber to endure and conquer the formidable challenges that the mountain presents.

The rewards of perseverance, nurtured by the art of patience, are abundant. As Pemba recounted his experiences, he described the profound joy of reaching the summit after days or even weeks of arduous climbing. He spoke of the serenity that comes from simply being present at the moment, surrounded by the breathtaking beauty of the snow-capped peaks and the vast expanse of untouched wilderness.

In the mountains, one learns that the journey is as significant as the destination. It is not merely about scaling a peak but the lessons learned along the way. Pemba Gelje's stories spoke of the countless hours spent trekking through rugged terrains, battling fatigue and facing physical and mental limitations. He taught me that every step forward, no matter how small, is a triumph. It is the embodiment of patience, the unwavering commitment to keep going despite the obstacles and uncertainties that lie ahead.

The mountains provide a powerful metaphor for life itself. They teach us that actual achievement does not come from fast-tracked success or instantaneous gratification. Instead, it stems from the willingness to embrace the art of patience, to take one step at a time, and to persevere even when the path seems treacherous and insurmountable. Pemba Gelje's journey, with its moments of triumph and introspection, serves as a testament to the rewards awaiting those who cultivate this virtue.

In witnessing Pemba Gelje's unwavering patience and resilience, I have come to understand that patience is not just the ability to wait but a way of approaching life, a state of being. It is about finding contentment in the present moment, basking in the beauty of the journey, and trusting that each small step will bring us closer to our goals.

As I continue to document Pemba Gelje's extraordinary life, I am reminded of the profound lessons he has imparted. The art of patience, learned from the mountains, has become a guiding principle in my life, weaving its way through the tapestry of my experiences. As I share Pemba Gelje's story with the world, I aim to inspire others to embrace this art, see the beauty in the slow and steady pace, and appreciate the rewards of persevering with unwavering patience.

Surrendering to Nature:

As a biographer and author, I have delved into the lives of individuals who have achieved incredible feats of courage, determination, and resilience. But as I embarked on the journey of capturing the energy of Pemba Gelje Sherpa, I soon realised that a unique theme loomed large in his story - the surrender required in the face of nature's power.

Nature is an entity that demands our utmost respect and reverence. The majestic mountains stand tall and sturdy, their peaks seemingly reaching out to touch the heavens. It is in the shadow of these formidable giants that human insignificance is laid bare. In the presence of such immense power, one cannot help but be humbled.

While researching this book, I stumbled upon stories of mountaineers who, despite their indomitable spirit, were forced to yield to the might of nature. Sherpas, who had dedicated their lives to guiding others through treacherous terrains, recounted stories of unexpected storms that ruthlessly stripped their strength and endurance. In these moments of surrender, they truly understood the fragility of human existence.

I remember Pemba sharing the story of his first encounter with the force of nature. A sudden blizzard engulfed their camp during one of his early expeditions to Everest. The howling winds threatened to rip apart their flimsy tents, and the biting cold pierced their bones with an unrelenting intensity. Pemba, a man who had spent his entire life amidst the mountains, thought he knew their power. But that night, as he huddled for shelter, he realised the futility of his knowledge.

Pemba learned an invaluable lesson in that moment of surrender - the mountains were not meant to be tamed, conquered, or challenged. They were meant to be respected and understood. A deep respect for the forces of nature began to permeate every fibre of his being. He no longer saw himself as a conqueror but as a conduit, a mere speck of dust in the vastness of the universe.

It is this surrender, this acceptance of our insignificance, that allows us to coexist with the majestic power of nature. We can only truly appreciate the beauty and grandeur surrounding us when we release our need for control. Pemba Gelje's experiences taught him that surrendering to nature does not equate to weakness or defeat but wisdom and reverence.

In our modern world, where autonomy and dominance are often valued above all else, Pemba Gelje's journey reminds us that forces beyond our control demand our surrender. And it is in this surrender, this surrender to nature, that we find a newfound freedom. A freedom that comes from embracing the unknown, acknowledging our limitations, and finding solace in the knowledge that we are but a small part of a larger tapestry.

As I continue to write the life story of Pemba Gelje Sherpa, I am reminded of the powerful lessons that surrendering to nature imparts. Through his unfathomable experiences in the mountains, he has taught me to let go of my ego and my need for control and to embrace the vastness and power of the natural world. It is a lesson that I want to convey to my readers that in surrendering to nature, we gain a deeper understanding of the world and ourselves.

Lessons in Gratitude:

As a biographer and author, I have spent my fair share of time delving into the lives of remarkable individuals. But never have I come across a story that so powerfully embodies the concept of gratitude as the life of Pemba Gelje Sherpa. Meeting him and hearing his stories of conquering mountains has illuminated the extraordinary feats of human strength and determination and instilled in me a deep appreciation for the simple blessings we often take for granted.

Pemba Gelje's physical and metaphorical journey has brought him face-to-face with nature's most majestic and formidable landscapes. As he recounts his mountaineering expeditions, he emphasises the overwhelming sense of humility and gratitude that the mountains have bestowed upon him. The sheer magnitude of these peaks demands respect and awe, reminding us of how insignificant our struggles and worries can be in the grand scheme of things.

Standing at the foot of these colossal giants, it is impossible not to feel a profound gratitude for life's blessings. The crisp mountain air fills your lungs, revitalising every cell in your body. The majestic beauty stretching out before you, untouched by the chaos of civilisation, serves as a reminder of the splendours of the natural world. Pemba often tells me that witnessing the sunrise from a mountain peak is a transcendental experience that imparts a deep gratitude for the gift of existence.

But it is not just the physical grandeur of the mountains that leaves an indelible mark on Pemba Gelje's soul. The people he has met and the lessons he has learned have genuinely shaped his perspective. Whether it is his fellow mountaineers, the Sherpa community he hails from, or the humble villagers he encounters during his expeditions, Pemba is grateful for the relationships he has formed and the invaluable wisdom they have imparted.

In this fast-paced world, where technology and material possessions seem to define success, it is easy to lose sight of the simple joys in life. But spending time with Pemba has reminded me of the importance of gratitude. The mountains have a unique way of stripping away the superficial, leaving us with a renewed appreciation for life's gifts. They remind us that success is not measured by the size of our bank accounts or the number of accolades we accumulate but by the depth of our relationships, the experiences that shape us, and the gratitude we show for it all.

So, as I continue to pen the story of Pemba Gelje Sherpa, I am reminded of the invaluable lessons he has taught me about gratitude. Through his experiences, I have realised that to appreciate the heights of happiness and fulfilment, we must first find gratitude in the simplicity of everyday life. Only then can we truly understand and cherish the blessings bestowed upon us and gain the perspective needed to conquer even the most unforgiving of mountains – both within ourselves and in the world around us.

CHAPTER 24
THE MOUNTAINS WITHIN US ALL

The Adventurous Spirit:

Pemba Gelje Sherpa's extraordinary life embodies this adventurous spirit. When I first encountered his story, I was captivated by his unwavering determination and boundless enthusiasm for exploration. Born and raised in the remote mountainous region of Nepal, Pemba was inherently drawn to the vastness of the natural world that surrounded him.

But what is it that ignites this adventurous spirit within us? Is it a genetic predisposition, an innate longing that transcends culture and upbringing? Or are life experiences pushing us to step outside our comfort zones and embrace the unknown?

In my research, I have discovered that the adventurous spirit resides within us, waiting to be awakened. It is a primal force connecting us to our ancestors, who ventured into uncharted territories in search of survival and prosperity. It is a fundamental part of our DNA, urging us to explore, to seek new horizons, and to challenge ourselves.

We need only look to history to witness the power of the adventurous spirit. From the ancient explorers who navigated treacherous seas in search of new lands to the astronauts who ventured beyond our atmosphere to touch the stars, it is evident that the yearning for exploration is deeply ingrained in our collective consciousness.

But how do we tap into this innate desire? How do we unlock the adventurous spirit within ourselves? The answer lies in embracing uncertainty and in adopting the unknown. We can awaken the dormant adventurer within by facing our fears, pushing past our perceived limitations, and embracing the thrill of venturing into uncharted territories.

For Pemba Gelje Sherpa, the call of the mountains was undeniable. From a young age, he felt a magnetic pull toward the peaks above his village. Overcoming physical and mental challenges, he scaled some of the highest and most treacherous mountains in the world, including Mount Everest itself.

Pemba Gelje's story is a testament to the transformative power of embracing our adventurous spirit and pushing the boundaries of our capabilities.

In my journey as a biographer, I have met countless individuals who have tapped into their own adventurous spirit. From artists who traverse uncharted creative territories to entrepreneurs who chart new paths in business, it is clear that the adventurous spirit manifests in many ways. What unites these individuals is their unwavering belief in their potential, refusal to settle for the ordinary, and willingness to take risks.

In conclusion, the adventurous spirit resides within us, beckoning us to explore the unknown, challenge our limits, and embrace the thrill of the journey. It is a force that cannot be ignored, for it is through embracing this innate desire that we come alive. Whether scaling great heights, charting new paths, or embarking on a personal voyage of self-discovery, let us heed the call of the adventurous spirit within and unlock the boundless potential within us all.

Climbing Our Personal Peaks:

As a biographer and author, my years of research and writing have brought me face-to-face with extraordinary individuals who have undertaken awe-inspiring journeys. Their experiences serve as a testament to the indomitable spirit within us all, urging us to overcome our metaphorical peaks.

In researching the life of Pemba Gelje Sherpa, I became enthralled with the parallels between his climbs in the Himalayas and the upgrades we all face. Pemba, an accomplished mountaineer, had conquered some of the most treacherous peaks known to humanity. Yet, not just his physical ascent intrigued me, but the mental, emotional, and spiritual obstacles he had to confront.

Like many of us, Pemba started his journey with lofty aspirations and a burning desire to reach the top. He possessed an unwavering determination and a relentless drive that pushed him forward, even when doubts started to creep in. I discovered that this resilience, this ability to push through adversity, was not innate but instead cultivated through a series of personal struggles. Pemba faced setbacks, failures, and moments of self-doubt, just as we all do.

In his quest to summit Mount Everest, Pemba confronted the harshest of conditions, battled altitude sickness, and faced the ever-looming threat of avalanches. These physical obstacles are undeniable, but his unwavering mindset struck me the most. Pemba possessed an unshakable belief in himself and his abilities, an idea that carried him through the dangers of high-altitude climbing and extended to the challenges he faced in his personal life.

As I dug deeper into Pemba Gelje's story, I discovered that his ability to conquer his personal mountains extended far beyond physicality. He tackled cultural expectations, societal norms, and the limitations imposed by his own self-doubt. Pemba demonstrated the courage to challenge the status quo and forge his path, inspiring others to do the same.

Our peaks may only sometimes involve literal mountains, but they are more demanding and formidable. They require us to confront our fears, push through physical and mental boundaries, and discover the strength within us that we may not have known existed. Just as Pemba had to acclimate to the thin air of the mountains, we must adapt to the unfamiliar, the uncomfortable, and the unknown.

In exploring Pemba Gelje Sherpa's life and his pursuit of conquering literal peaks, I understand that our personal summits are not confined to grand expeditions. They are accessible to all of us, regardless of our circumstances or past. The mindset we cultivate, the resilience we foster, and the unwavering belief in ourselves enable us to embark on our own journeys of self-discovery and personal growth.

So, let us embrace the metaphorical mountains in our lives, facing them head-on with courage and determination. Let us traverse unknown terrain, navigate treacherous slopes, and find solace in the knowledge that, just like Pemba Gelje Sherpa, we, too, can climb our peaks. With each step, we inch closer to the summit, where we will find a breathtaking view and the triumph of knowing we have conquered our mountains.

The Call of the Mountains:

The whisper of the mountains is an irresistible force that beckons even the most reluctant souls. It is not simply the physical allure, the majestic beauty that captivates us, but something deeper, something intangible. It is as if the mountains possess an otherworldly power that resonates with our essence, stirring emotions and igniting a longing to explore the unknown.

In the quiet moments of solitude amidst the peaks, one can witness the true power of this call. It transcends language and culture, touching the deepest recesses of our souls. The mountains have borne witness to the dreams and aspirations of countless individuals, acting as both a canvas for our human desires and a mirror that reflects our innermost selves.

Each mountain range has its unique character and story to tell. From the rugged peaks of the Himalayas to the snow-dusted summits of the Rockies, these giants of nature have witnessed the triumphs and defeats of human endeavour. They have seen explorers push the boundaries of what was possible, battling the elements and their limitations. They have witnessed the sacrifices made to pursue glory and the ultimate desire to conquer the heights.

To embrace the mountains within ourselves is to embrace the challenge, the unpredictability, and the raw beauty they offer. It is to acknowledge our vulnerabilities and fears and confront them head-on. The mountains teach us resilience, pushing us to dig deeper into our reserves of strength and determination. They force us to confront our limitations, revealing the true extent of our capabilities.

But it is not just about conquering the physical summit but the journey itself. The mountains have a way of stripping away the distractions of our modern lives, allowing us to reconnect with the essence of our being. In their vastness, we find a sense of perspective, realising our place within the grand tapestry of nature.

In the face of the mountains, we are humbled. We are reminded of our smallness in the grand scheme of things yet inspired by the endless possibilities. The mountains teach us that there is always more to discover and more to explore. They beckon us to go beyond our comfort zones and embrace the unknown, for growth and transformation genuinely occur in these moments of uncertainty.

As I delve deeper into the stories of those who have answered the call, I am constantly reminded of the enduring allure of the mountains. It is a call that transcends time and space, resonating with the very core of our human existence. It is a call that cannot be ignored; to ignore it is to deny a part of ourselves.

So, I embark on this literary journey, guided by the call of the mountains, eager to uncover the hidden stories within their mighty peaks. As I document the triumphs and tribulations of those who have ventured into the unknown, I aim to convey the magnitude of their experiences and inspire others to embrace the mountains within themselves. The call of the mountains is a call that cannot be silenced; it is a call that resonates with every one of us, urging us to chase our dreams and discover the heights that await us.

CHAPTER 25
A LOVE LETTER
TO THE MOUNTAINS

Words That Fall Short :

Throughout my research, I have stumbled upon countless attempts to describe the grandeur and majesty of these towering giants. Poets have penned sonnets, writers have woven intricate narratives, and adventurers have shared awe-inspiring stories. And while some have come close to conveying the magnificence of these natural wonders, all inevitably need to capture the essence at the heart of these mountains truly.

The vocabulary at my disposal seems meagre in the face of the boundless awe and wonder inspired by the mountains. How does one articulate the feeling of standing at the foot of a colossal peak, the air crisp and thin, the immensity of the landscape stretching out before you in a breathtaking panorama?

There is a certain magic in the mountains – a mystical quality that defies explanation. Like attempting to hold a handful of mist, the ineffable qualities of these majestic giants slip through the grasp of words. The ethereal dance of light on a snow-covered summit, the deafening silence that envelops you at higher altitudes, and the impenetrable serenity that embraces you as you traverse remote valleys – these moments elude description.

In my quest to tell Pemba Gelje Sherpa's story, I have ventured into territories where language trembles on the precipice of its limitations. How can I genuinely convey the determination and resilience that fueled his ascent? How can I articulate the searing cold and biting wind that carved its way into his bones as he ascended treacherous slopes? These experiences are deeply personal and transcend the confines of words.

Yet, in acknowledging these limitations, I am undeterred in my attempt to express the inexpressible. While words may fall short, they possess the power to ignite the imaginations of those who yearn to understand the invisible threads that bind us to these ancient peaks. Through my storytelling, I aim to evoke the essence of Pemba Gelje Sherpa's journey, inspiring readers to venture into the untamed wilderness and seek their own connection with the mountains.

Though I may struggle to encapsulate the full breadth of the mountains' beauty, my commitment as a writer remains resolute. I will transcend the limitations of language, weaving a tapestry of words that invites readers to glimpse the indescribable. For in those fleeting moments where my words resonate and stir emotions, I will implore readers to join Pemba Gelje Sherpa on a remarkable expedition, where life and death dance on the razor's edge, and the mountains reveal truths that exist far beyond the grasp of mere language.

A Symphony of Gratitude:

In my pursuit of unravelling Pemba Gelje's enigma, I am struck by a recurring theme in his life - an unwavering and boundless gratitude. It is a symphony, a crescendo of reverence, that he plays to the mountains, the lessons he has learned, the joy he has experienced, and the deep sense of fulfilment from a life spent in their formidable presence.

The majestic and unyielding mountains have been Pemba Gelje's steadfast companions throughout his existence. From the moment he took his first steps as a child, nestled among the towering peaks of the Himalayas, he felt their magnetic pull. Their grandeur and awe-inspiring beauty seeped into his very being, shaping his perspective and instilling profound respect in him. Pemba expresses his gratitude to these towering giants, for they have shown him the way, challenged him to push beyond his limits, and offered him solace in times of uncertainty.

But gratitude does not stop at the mountains themselves; it extends to the lessons gleaned from their rugged slopes. Pemba has traversed treacherous paths, weathered storms, and faced unimaginable obstacles. Yet, with each trial and tribulation, he discovered a reservoir of inner strength that he never knew existed. He is indebted to these lessons, for they have allowed him to stand tall amidst adversity and navigate the twists and turns of life's unpredictable journey.

Pemba Gelje's symphony of gratitude also resounds with the infectious joy he has found in the outdoors. Whether it be scaling a sheer cliff face, breathing in the crisp mountain air, or witnessing the breathtaking sunrise painting the snow-capped peaks in myriad colours, his heart overflows with a joy that cannot be contained. This joy is reserved for himself and extended to those who have accompanied him on his expeditions, for Pemba understands that true happiness multiplies when shared.

Yet, beyond the mountains, the lessons, and the joy, Pemba Gelje's boundless gratitude swells from the depths of his soul due to the deep sense of fulfilment he has found in a life dedicated to the mountains. The hills have been a backdrop and a way of life for Pemba. Each step, each breath, and each moment spent in their presence has brought him closer to his true self. It is a precious gift that he cherishes, and he expresses his gratitude by living every day to the fullest, seeking out new adventures, and honouring the mountains that have shaped his identity.

In the symphony of gratitude that Pemba Gelje Sherpa exudes, I am a captive audience, mesmerised by the harmonious blend of reverence, humility, and awe that permeates his being. His story transcends words and reaches into the very depths of our souls, reminding us to express our gratitude to the mountains, the lessons learned, the joy experienced, and the deep sense of fulfilment that comes from immersing ourselves in the wonders of nature.

Forever Bound:

As a biographer and author, my journey with Pemba Gelje Sherpa has been filled with awe and reverence for the majestic mountains that have shaped his life. Through countless interviews and hours spent researching and documenting his adventures, I have understood the profound bond he shares with the hills – a bond forged in sweat, tears, and a deep respect for the natural world.

Pemba Gelje's love for the mountains began as a young boy, growing up amidst the towering peaks of the Himalayas. He would often marvel at their grandeur, feeling an inexplicable pull that would eventually define the course of his life. It was as if these majestic monoliths were beckoning him, whispering stories of adventure and daring.

Pemba would venture into the mountains in his early climbing career with trepidation and excitement. Each step was a test of courage, a push beyond his physical limits, and a constant reminder of his mortality. Yet, amidst the unpredictable weather, the treacherous terrain, and the ever-present danger, he found solace in the mountains. It was as if they offered him a sanctuary where he could confront his fears, challenge his boundaries, and find his true self.

Mountaineering has a certain magic – a dance between man and mountain that transcends time and space. It is a delicate balance of power and vulnerability, strength and humility. In the face of a towering peak, one must surrender to its might, recognising that nature is the ultimate authority. And yet, in this surrender, the mountaineer discovers their strength, resilience, and ability to thrive amidst chaos.

Pemba often speaks of the profound sense of peace he experiences in the mountains. In the quiet solitude of a summit, he finds a connection to something greater than himself. It is as if time stands still, and he becomes part of the eternal tapestry that has unfolded for millennia. The mountains, with their towering peaks and sweeping valleys, offer a glimpse into the vastness of the universe, reminding Pemba of his place within it.

But it is not just the physicality of mountaineering that captivates Pemba. It is also the community that thrives within this realm. The mountaineering fraternity is a tight-knit family – a band of individuals who share a common passion for the outdoors and a deep respect for the mountains. They understand the risks, the sacrifices, and the unparalleled joy that comes with conquering a summit. It is a brotherhood and sisterhood that transcends language, culture, and nationality. It is a bond formed in the crucible of adversity, where trust and dependability hold the power to preserve life.

Reflecting on Pemba Gelje's journey, I am struck by his enduring love affair with the mountains. It is a love that cannot be easily defined or contained, for it encompasses many emotions – from fear and exhilaration to awe and respect. It is a love that is fierce, delicate, consuming, and nurturing. It is a love that defies the constraints of time and space, and it is a love that will never fade.

As I continue exploring Pemba Gelje's life and achievements, I am reminded of the timeless bond between mountaineer and mountain. This bond transcends the physical and reaches the depths of the soul. It is a bond formed through perseverance, determination and an unwavering belief in the human spirit. This bond has shaped Pemba into the extraordinary individual he is today – a man forever bound to the mountains he loves.

CHAPTER 26
THE SPIRIT OF ADVENTURE

Embracing the Unknown:

In my pursuit of capturing untold stories and hidden narratives, I have witnessed how delving into the unknown can be terrifying and exhilarating. As individuals, we naturally seek comfort and security within the confines of familiarity. We construct our lives within neat boundaries, creating an illusion of control. Yet, when we step outside our comfort zones, we come alive in those fleeting moments.

When I think of embracing the unknown, I cannot help but be reminded of the courageous exploits of Pemba Gelje Sherpa. Pemba was a remarkable individual, a mountaineer who had dedicated his life to exploring the untouched peaks of the Himalayas. His unwavering determination and relentless pursuit of the unexplored fascinated me from the moment I first discovered his story.

In his eyes, the unknown was not something to be feared but embraced with open arms. It was a challenge to be conquered, an opportunity to test his limits, and a gateway to unimagined possibilities. The sheer audacity of his adventures left me in awe and ignited a burning desire to understand what drives individuals like Pemba to delve into the depths of the unknown.

As a biographer, I embarked on an intensive research journey to uncover the secrets behind Pemba Gelje's relentless pursuit of the unknown. I spoke to family members, friends, and fellow mountaineers who had witnessed his endeavours firsthand. Their stories painted a vivid picture of a man fueled by an insatiable curiosity and an unquenchable thirst for discovery.

Through my research, I discovered that embracing the unknown requires unique qualities – resilience, adaptability, and an unyielding belief in oneself. It is not for the faint of heart nor for those seeking comfort and stability at every turn. But the rewards are immeasurable for those who dare to venture into uncharted territories.

The rewards of embracing the unknown extend far beyond personal achievement. In moments of uncertainty and self-discovery, we find our most authentic selves. We are pushed to our limits, forced to confront our fears, and empowered to overcome obstacles that once seemed impossible. The unknown becomes the canvas on which our deepest strengths are unveiled and our most profound growth occurs.

In the world of exploration, the allure of the unknown lies not only in the physical landscapes that await us but also in the endless possibilities that reside within our minds. The uncharted territories of our dreams and aspirations beckon us to step outside of our comfort zones and embrace a life lived fully.

As I continue delving into the story of Pemba Gelje Sherpa, I am reminded of the beauty and significance of embracing the unknown. It is a reminder that life's most incredible adventures often lie just beyond the familiar, waiting to be discovered by those audacious enough to leap. And it is in that leap that we find the thrill of exploration and the transformative power of embracing our true potential.

The Journey Never Ends:

Exploring the never-ending nature of the journey is an essential theme that reverberates throughout Pemba Gelje's life. He embodies the spirit of constant pursuit, forever seeking new horizons to conquer and fueled by an insatiable thirst for exploration. To understand Pemba Gelje's unwavering confidence, one must delve into the core of his being, tracing the roots of his ancestral heritage.

Born into a lineage of sherpas, Pemba grew up in the majestic shadow of the Himalayas, his backyard an altar of breathtaking peaks, frozen rivers, and ancient glaciers. The very geography of his homeland breathed adventure into his veins as he marvelled at the snow-capped giants that seemed to beckon him closer with their icy fingertips. It was within this awe-inspiring landscape that Pemba Gelje's journey began, a journey that would extend far beyond the boundaries of his earthly surroundings.

From a tender age, Pemba found solace in nature's embrace, finding comfort in the silence of pristine mountains and the untamed wilderness. Every peak he scaled, every ice wall he conquered, and every trail he treaded brought him one step closer to understanding the boundless nature of the human spirit. Each expedition became a stepping stone towards self-discovery, a testament to the indomitable will that burned within him.

But it was not just the physical aspect of exploration that captivated Pemba. He recognised that the journey was not confined to the external realm alone; it was a continuous excavation of the soul, an unending quest for personal growth and enlightenment. With each passing traverse of unforgiving landscapes, Pemba peeled away layers of himself, shedding the fears, insecurities, and limitations that shackled him to the mundane.

Indeed, the journey never ends for Pemba. It is not marked by finite destinations or culminating achievements but rather by the perpetual yearning to traverse uncharted territories within and without. It is a dance with the unknown, an intimate tango with the mysteries of life, and an acknowledgement that growth stems from venturing beyond the boundaries of comfort.

Pemba Gelje's relentless pursuit of new horizons is rooted in an innate desire to defy the constraints of perceived limitations, shatter boundaries, and transcend boundaries of what is possible. He embodies the essence of the human spirit, for he relentlessly strives to push the limits of human potential, inspiring others to embrace their powers of resilience and embark on their unique odysseys.

As I continue to unravel the intricacies of his journey, I am acutely aware that my relationship with Pemba is not confined to the transient pages of a book. No, it is a symbiotic connection that weaves the threads of two narratives into a fabric that binds us eternally. Together, we embark on an odyssey of discovery, where the journey never truly ends but instead serves as a reminder that life's most profound meaning lies not in the destination but in the magnificent tapestry of experiences that we weave as we venture forth into the great unknown.

Beyond the Summits:

Mountains have always fascinated me. Their majestic beauty, towering peaks, and rugged landscapes inspire awe and admiration. They have always represented a symbol of challenge, resilience, and the human spirit's indomitable will to conquer the impossible. Through my research, I have come to appreciate the physical and mental demands of mountaineering. It is a realm of ceaseless struggle, where climbers push themselves to their limits, battling freezing temperatures, thin air, and treacherous terrain.

But there is something more to mountaineering than merely reaching the summit. It is a transformative experience that extends far beyond the physical realm. The mountains serve as a backdrop for a deeper exploration of the self, a journey of introspection and self-discovery. The quiet solitude amidst the majestic peaks allows for contemplation and reflection, stripping away the layers of societal expectations and revealing the essence of one's being.

As I continue to delve into Pemba Gelje's life, I am captivated by the depths of his spirit, the strength of his character, and the unwavering determination that propelled him forward. His story is not just about conquering mountains; it is about beating the limitations of one's mind and finding solace in the unknown. Pemba Gelje's relentless pursuit of his dreams reminds us that there is always more to explore beyond the summits we have already conquered.

In researching Pemba Gelje's expeditions, I have stumbled upon an untold world of adventure waiting to be discovered. Remote mountain ranges, hidden valleys, and unexplored peaks beckon to those willing to venture beyond the familiar. These uncharted territories are not limited to the physical realm but extend to the domains of art, technology, science, and the limitless human imagination.

As a biographer, I must present Pemba Gelje's story in all its grandeur to give readers a glimpse into the world of mountaineering and the invaluable life lessons it bestows upon those who dare to venture into its realms. But I realise that there is more to be done. Pemba Gelje's narrative is a stepping stone, a catalyst for further exploration and contemplation. It is an invitation to look beyond the summits and discover the vast expanse of possibilities within ourselves and in the unexplored territories of the world.

In the following pages, join me as we embark on an expedition of the mind, a journey that will take us far beyond the peaks that Pemba has conquered. Together, let us delve into the boundless possibilities as we explore the uncharted territories of our dreams, passions, and potential. It is a journey that promises to be both exhilarating and transformative, offering us a glimpse into the untapped depths of our souls and the wonders that await us in the world around us.

So, let us set aside our preconceived notions, embrace the unknown, and embark on this voyage of self-discovery. For beyond the summits lie the treasures of life, waiting patiently for us to uncover them. Let us strap on our backpacks and set off into the horizon, for the adventure of a lifetime begins now.

CHAPTER 27
THE POWER OF
HUMAN CONNECTION

The Strength of Unity:

In the towering peaks of the Himalayas, where danger lurks at every step and the whims of nature can be erratic, unity becomes an essential lifeline. Pemba Gelje Sherpa, a renowned mountaineer from the Sherpa community, epitomises the indomitable spirit of unity within this daunting arena. Through his experiences, I have witnessed firsthand the transformative effects of collaborative effort and shared determination.

I vividly recall one particular expedition where Pemba and his team tackled the treacherous slopes of Everest. It was a gruelling undertaking, with each team member tethered to one another for safety. As they ascended, they realised their combined strength and courage were vital to their success. The intricate dance of trust and support unfolded as they traversed icy crevasses and navigated perilous ridges.

In the face of adversity, the collective spirit shone through. Each climber became not just an individual striving for personal accomplishment but an indispensable cog in a well-oiled machine. Their forged bond transformed them into a unified force, powerfully propelling them towards their shared objective. They pushed themselves beyond their perceived limits, drawing upon the power of unity to overcome physical and mental obstacles.

However, the strength of unity is more than just the physical challenges encountered in the mountains. It extends beyond the routinely unpredictable weather and the ever-present risk of avalanches. It permeates the very essence of the climbing community, becoming a cornerstone of their shared identity and purpose. Support networks emerge, friendships are forged, and a collective goal envelops every climber.

In the depths of hardship, unity becomes a bedrock of emotional sustenance. When faced with exhausting altitude sickness, bone-chilling cold, or severe exhaustion, the unwavering support of fellow climbers fuels the spirit and lifts weary hearts. It is a cohesion borne out of a shared commitment to overcome adversity, a pact to rise above the challenges that nature throws their way.

As I continued to research and document climbers' experiences like Pemba Gelje Sherpa, I became enthralled by the innate resilience and camaraderie that binds them. Their stories test what can be achieved when individuals unite behind a common goal, breaking through limits and defying the constraints of the human body.

In the mountains, the strength of unity reveals itself in a magnificent symphony of cooperation and selflessness. It is a force that propels climbers to ever-greater heights, transcending the boundaries of individual capability. It is a reminder that when we stand together, bound by the ties of shared ambition and unwavering camaraderie, we can achieve extraordinary feats. And in the case of mountaineers like Pemba Gelje Sherpa, their relentless pursuit of greatness is a testament to unity's power in all its awe-inspiring glory.

Climbing Together:

As a biographer and author, I have spent countless hours delving into the lives of extraordinary individuals. However, none have fascinated me, like Pemba Gelje Sherpa, the mountaineer from the Himalayas. Throughout my research, I encountered numerous stories of breathtaking climbs, daring achievements, and unbelievable feats of survival. But one aspect that continuously emerged was the profound impact that climbing had on Pemba Gelje's relationships and the incredible bond between climbers on the mountains.

Mountaineering, by its very nature, requires individuals to depend on one another for survival. In a world where nature reigns supreme, and the slightest mistake can lead to disaster, climbers instinctively come together, relying on each other's strengths, skills, and experience. It is these moments of unity that not only forge lifelong friendships but create a profound sense of camaraderie and trust.

As I discovered, Pemba was no stranger to these connections' significance. His climbing partners were not simply comrades; they were his family, his confidants, and his support system. Together, they formed a tightly knit group, bound by a shared purpose and driven by a mutual desire to conquer mountains that seemed impossible to others.

One particular climb that exemplified this extraordinary bond was a summit attempt on Mount Everest. Pemba and his team found themselves battling extreme weather conditions, treacherous terrain, and their own physical limitations. Long before dawn, they climbed in unison, each step bringing them closer to their shared goal. Their collective determination provided the fuel that kept them going, even when fatigue threatened to consume them. In those moments, words were unnecessary; a glance or a reassuring touch was all that was needed to communicate their unyielding support for one another.

Throughout the arduous climb, I witnessed a camaraderie that went beyond ordinary human interactions. It was as though these climbers had developed a language of their own, an unspoken understanding that enabled them to navigate the harshest conditions. They moved in perfect synchrony, trusting their fellow climbers to guide them through the treacherous paths and to lend a helping hand when needed.

But it wasn't just on the mountains that these enduring connections were forged; it was in the shared experiences etched into their memories forever. The hours spent huddled together in impromptu campsites, cooking simple but nourishing meals, and sharing laughter and stories served as the foundation for friendships that would span a lifetime. They were moments when stripped away from the distractions of the modern world, climbers discovered the true essence of human connection.

This unique facet of mountaineering sets it apart from any other adventure. In adversity, climbers find solace and strength in their shared experiences. With all its grandeur and challenges, the mountain becomes a catalyst for deepening human relationships, creating connections that withstand the test of time.

As I delved deeper into Pemba Gelje Sherpa's life, I marvelled at the remarkable bonds he had formed on the mountains and their profound impact on his personal growth. Through their shared triumphs and occasional heartaches, Pemba Gelje's climbing partners had become an integral part of his narrative, shaping him into the extraordinary individual he was.

In mountaineering, the pursuit of summits becomes secondary to the lifelong connections formed along the way. These connections weave a vibrant tapestry, drawing climbers together from different corners of the world, bridging cultures and backgrounds, and revealing the extraordinary power of human connection in the face of nature's most significant challenges.

One Mountain, One World:

Mountains have an uncanny ability to transcend geographical boundaries and cultural differences. They become a unifying force that brings people together, forging connections between individuals who may have never crossed paths. The mountaineering community is an intricate tapestry woven with threads of diverse backgrounds, languages, and experiences. Yet, on the slopes of these awe-inspiring giants, we all converge, communicating not through words but through a common language—the language of the mountains.

In this global community, nationality, ethnicity, and social status become secondary to the shared experience of immersing oneself in the untamed beauty and raw power of Mother Nature's masterpieces. From the Himalayas' peaks to the Andes' summits, mountaineers navigate the same treacherous icefalls, endure the same bone-chilling blizzards, and face the same towering obstacles that test their physical and mental limits. It is a language understood by all who tread these hallowed grounds, transcending the barriers of language, culture, and ideology.

However, not only the challenges and risks unite these intrepid adventurers. A deep reverence and respect for the mountainous landscapes permeates the mountaineering community. Each climber understands they are merely guests in this sacred realm, and they are responsible for leaving no trace of their passage. Whether Sherpa, European, or American, all adventurers converge on a shared code of ethics—leave the mountain as you found it, preserving the pristine wilderness for generations to come.

This shared love and respect for the mountains is a bond that cannot be broken. It forms the foundation of a global movement dedicated to conservation and preservation. Mountaineers have witnessed firsthand the devastating effects of climate change on these fragile ecosystems and are at the forefront of efforts to combat it. Through their expeditions and personal stories, they inspire millions worldwide to protect these majestic peaks and the delicate balance of nature.

As I reflect on the intricacies of the mountaineering community and the profound unity it fosters, I am left in awe of its power. Pemba Gelje Sherpa, like so many mountaineers before him, stands as a testament to the indomitable human spirit and the unifying force that one mountain can have on a world divided by so many things. It is an enduring reminder that despite our differences, constants bind us all—a love for nature, an appreciation for the awe-inspiring, and a shared responsibility to protect and preserve our planet. In the face of one mountain, we become one world.

CHAPTER 28
THE ENDLESS SUMMITS

Pemba, a man of few words but boundless passion, was drawn to the mountains from a young age. His unwavering commitment to his Sherpa heritage and the sacred land he belonged to was evident even in his earliest days. Growing up in a small Sherpa village nestled among towering peaks, he witnessed the austere beauty of the landscape and felt an inexplicable connection deep within his soul. It was a calling, an indescribable force that compelled him to hold the mountains close to his heart forever.

From his first ascent of a modest hill to his treacherous encounters with the world's highest summits, Pemba Gelje's love for the mountains grew stronger. With every step he took, every breath of thin air he inhaled, he revelled in the raw majesty surrounding him. The hills offered solace in their vastness, a sanctuary where he could find comfort and purpose. They were his refuge, his teacher, and his ultimate challenge.

In the face of adversities and dangers that would deter the faint-hearted, Pemba pressed on, his resolve unwavering. He endured the bone-chilling cold, the treacherous icefalls, and the ever-present threat of avalanches. Yet, amidst it all, he found solace. The mountains taught him perseverance, humility, and resilience. Each setback he encountered became a stepping stone in his journey towards self-discovery.

But it was not merely conquering mountains that fueled Pemba Gelje's passion; it was the bond he formed with nature and the spiritual awakening he experienced in its presence. He immersed himself in the culture, traditions, and rituals of the Sherpa people, cherishing the ancient wisdom passed down from generation to generation. Through the mountains, Pemba found a connection to something greater than himself.

His devotion to the mountains went beyond personal fulfilment; it extended to his community and people. Ever grateful for the opportunities his beloved mountains had provided him, Pemba dedicated himself to ensuring a brighter future for the Sherpa community. He mentored younger Sherpas, sharing his knowledge and expertise with a selflessness characteristic of his nature. Pemba understood that the mountains belonged not only to him but to all who sought their solace.

As I reflect on Pemba Gelje's extraordinary life, I am struck by the mountains' profound impact on him. The call of the mountains was not merely a fleeting desire but a lifelong commitment. It was an unbreakable bond that endured until the end of his days, transcending time and space. Pemba Gelje's legacy will forever be intertwined with the majestic peaks he passionately embraced.

In writing Pemba Gelje Sherpa's biography, I have come to understand the power of the mountains and the magnetic pull they exert on the hearts and souls of those who dare to answer their call. Pemba Gelje's journey is not just a story of triumph over physical challenges; it is a testament to the transformative power of nature and the indomitable spirit of the human soul. Through Pemba Gelje's story, I strive to honour the mountains and inspire others to heed their own call, wherever it may lead.

The Legacy Lives On:

Having spent countless hours researching and documenting Pemba Gelje's life, I have understood the profound significance of his mountaineering achievements. Pemba Gelje's name has become synonymous with perseverance, strength, and the indomitable human spirit, leaving an indelible mark on the mountaineering world.

His early years in the Sherpa community made him a resilient and tenacious individual. Growing up surrounded by the towering peaks of the Himalayas, Pemba Gelje's passion for mountaineering was ignited from an early age. To witness a young boy from a humble background rise to conquer some of the world's highest mountains is awe-inspiring.

A series of groundbreaking accomplishments characterised Pemba Gelje's mountaineering career. From his successful summit of Everest at the tender age of 19 to his remarkable ascent of K2, each achievement pushed the boundaries of what was considered possible in mountaineering. Pemba paved the way for future climbers, demonstrating that the seemingly impossible could be conquered with determination and skill.

But beyond his physical feats, Pemba Gelje's legacy lies in his unwavering commitment to his Sherpa community. He recognised the need for change and tirelessly advocated for better working conditions for his fellow Sherpas. Pemba Gelje's efforts helped bring attention to the challenges faced by Sherpa climbers, leading to significant improvements in safety and working conditions in the mountains.

Furthermore, Pemba Gelje's mountaineering accomplishments inspired a new generation of climbers to pursue their dreams. His story motivated young Sherpas and climbers from all walks of life to believe in their abilities and strive for greatness. Pemba Gelje's legacy is not only about his achievements but also about the hope he instilled in others, fueling their mountaineering aspirations.

As a biographer and author, I am privileged to continue sharing Pemba Gelje's story. Through his journey, readers can gain a profound understanding of the power of the human spirit and the immense beauty of the natural world. Pemba Gelje's legacy constantly reminds us of the limitless potential within each of us.

In conclusion, Pemba Gelje Sherpa's mountainous path may have ended, but his legacy lives on. His profound impact on mountaineering, his advocacy for the Sherpa community, and the inspiration he has sparked in countless individuals will forever leave an indelible mark on climbing. Pemba Gelje's story will continue to inspire and captivate climbers for generations to come, ensuring that his legacy lives on eternally in the hearts and minds of those who dare to dream.

Forever in the Mountains :

From the moment he first set foot on the rugged terrain of the Himalayas, Pemba felt an inexplicable pull that defied logic. It was as if the mountains, with their majestic peaks and awe-inspiring landscapes, whispered secrets into his soul. The essence of his being seemed to sync with the rhythm of nature, forever entwined with the mighty earth that stretched up to the heavens.

In the silence of the mountains, so distant from the clamour of civilisation, Pemba discovered a sense of serenity that words alone cannot capture. It was an unspoken understanding, a communion between man and nature, where the mountains revealed their timeless wisdom to him alone. The jagged peaks and treacherous slopes became his teachers, patiently guiding him along winding trails as he absorbed their lessons.

Embracing this eternal connection, Pemba knew that his spirit would forever reside amongst the peaks. It was a strong, unbreakable bond that not even death itself could sever. As he climbed higher, pushing his physical and mental limits, he carried the collective dreams, aspirations, and fearless spirit of his Sherpa ancestors. They, too, had engraved their presence upon the mountains, leaving an indelible mark that echoed through the ages.

The realm beyond the earthly realm beckoned Pemba with promises of endless summits, a world where the boundaries of mortality dissolved, and the pursuit of elevation knew no bounds. He yearned to ascend to peaks untouched by human feet, challenge the limits of his being, and soar amidst the clouds with the freedom that only the mountains could bestow.

But it was not a quest fueled by ego or a desire for personal glory. No, his ambitions were founded on a profound reverence for the mountains.

Pemba understood that to conquer a peak was not to conquer nature but to earnestly listen to her whispers and embrace the grandeur of the universe.

With every step he took, Pemba embodied the spirit of adventure and exploration within each of us. He taught us that it is not the destination that shapes our journey but the courage to embark upon it. With their stoic presence and infinite splendour, the mountains became both his sanctuary and his muse, inspiring him to reach insurmountable heights.

And so, as I reflect upon Pemba Gelje Sherpa's profound connection with the mountains, I am reminded of the power within us all. We, too, can embrace the eternal call of the peaks and discover the boundless horizons that whisper our name with each ascent, for it is in the mountains that we find our most authentic selves, forever woven into the tapestry of nature, forever seeking the summits that await in the realm beyond.

CHAPTER 29
FROZEN IN TIME

'Entombed in Ice: A Profound Reflection from the Heart of Everest'
Direct from Pemba Gelje Sherpa:

As I ascend into the unforgiving embrace of Mount Everest, a sad reflection envelops me. This towering sentinel of ice and rock has witnessed countless adventurers scaling its treacherous heights, each seeking a fleeting moment of triumph captured in a selfie or a high-five. Yet, amidst these victories lies a chilling truth—hundreds have never tasted that summit glory; the mountain has claimed them.

The words of George Mallory from 1924 echo in my mind: 'But when I say our sport is a hazardous one, I do not mean that when we climb mountains, there is a large chance that we shall be killed, but that we are surrounded by dangers which will kill us if we let them.'

Mount Everest, touted as the world's tallest peak, holds another, more macabre title: the world's largest open-air graveyard.

No one can quantify the exact number of souls who remain entwined with Everest, but their number exceeds 200. Climbers and Sherpas lie at rest, hidden in crevasses, entombed beneath snow avalanches, or eerily exposed on the mountain's slopes—their once-daring limbs now bleached and contorted by the elements. Some remain shrouded in mystery, while others have become melancholic landmarks on the path to Everest's summit. I have crossed paths with one such figure significantly in my journeys, a nameless adventurer who followed his dream into eternity. I bow my head in silent tribute each time I pass.

One of the mountain's most haunting legends is that of Tsewang Paljor, remembered as 'Green Boots' among seasoned climbers for the fluorescent footwear he wore during his fatal climb in the notorious 1996 blizzard. For nearly two decades, Green Boots has maintained his frozen vigil near Everest's north side summit, his outstretched legs an ominous threshold for those ascending and descending.

The apex of Everest, above 26,000 feet, is the perilous 'death zone.' There, oxygen levels plummet to a third of those at sea level, and barometric pressure makes every step feel ten times heavier. It induces lethargy, disorientation, and organ failure, often culminating in death. In this realm, survival rarely extends beyond 48 hours. Those who succumb are left where they fell, serving as haunting signposts for future climbers.

While mountaineers like myself regard these tragedies as heartbreaking yet inevitable, the idea of a body enduring for nearly two decades in plain sight baffles the human psyche. Will these souls rest eternally on Everest's unforgiving slopes, or can we do more? Will we ever reach the point where we deem Everest unworthy? For now, my belief is steadfast: Everest remains a story of control, danger, mourning, and revelations.

However, I hold one conviction—Everest is no longer the untouched, romantic frontier it once was. Since Tenzing Norgay and Edmund Hillary's historic ascent in 1953, over 7,000 summits by more than 4,000 individuals have scarred the mountain, leaving litter, human waste, and bodies. As one who treads upon this sacred ground year after year, I do my part by collecting the refuse left by those who have not revered the mountain they march. Yet, a few guardians are insufficient to maintain Everest's purity. Lucrative opportunities entice us, the Sherpas and me, but motivations remain an enigma for others. Many profes-sional climbers assert their drive differs from those of clients who pay for bragging rights. Yet, it's undeniable that some see Everest as a vanity project, a race for records, an insult to the mountain's spiritual essence.

The tragedy of David Sharp underscores this shift in climbers' attitudes. In 2006, Sharp, attempting to summit alone, met his demise in Green Boots' cave. Over several agonising hours, he succumbed to the cold within sight of the world's most renowned Everest casualty. Unlike Green Boots, who likely perished unnoticed during a less crowded era, at least 40 climbers passed Sharp that fateful day. Eyewitnesses attest that he was alive and in distress. None stopped. None extended a helping hand. I find this unfathomable and revolting—an indictment of humanity's callousness.

I would have stopped, as my role as a mountain guardian and as a fellow human compelled me to aid anyone in distress. Basic decency eludes some. Sir Edmund Hillary, the pioneer of Everest, criticised those who passed Sharp, attributing their actions to a mindless obsession with reaching the summit. He remarked, 'The people just want to get to the top. They don't give a damn for anybody else who may be in distress, and it doesn't impress me at all that they leave someone lying under a rock to die.' This phenomenon was termed 'summit fever,' a dark undercurrent in Everest's history.

Psychologists have endeavoured to dissect the motivations of professional climbers, defining them as sensation-seekers thriving on thrill. Yet, climbing Everest is a gruelling journey, a relentless battle against exhaustion and discomfort. However, one's mind operates, Everest's symbolism captivates, whether as a crucible of transformation, a conquest over personal demons, or the pinnacle of a lifelong pursuit.

Yet, it pains me to admit that Everest's sanctity diminishes with each passing year. The mountain bears witness to a constant stream of climbers, driven by a spectrum of motives, leaving behind scars and stories that tarnish its once-pristine majesty. Like many, I climb for personal and intrinsic reasons, but the spiritual essence of these peaks must not be compromised. They offer a privilege, a chance to touch the heavens, to cleanse our souls, and to reconnect with nature. Everest's hallowed ground deserves respect, not exploitation. While records may fall, let us remember the sacredness of these heights.

For now, people will continue to ascend Everest, braving its dangers, and many will become eternal sentinels of ice. Their stories remain frozen in time, warning us of the price of hubris and beckoning us to reflect on the ever-changing face of Everest.

CHAPTER 30
THE FROZEN SOULS
WHO DESERVE RESPECT

As a biographer and author, I have always been drawn to the stories within the deepest recesses of the human experience. And few stories are as hauntingly captivating as those of the frozen souls on Mount Everest or any other mountain. With its treacherous slopes and unpredictable weather, the mountain has claimed the lives of over 300 climbers in recent history, leaving behind a chilling reminder of the risks taken in pursuit of greatness.

It is estimated that about two-thirds of these fallen climbers still rest on Everest, their bodies frozen in time. The current count of souls that need to be retrieved from the mountain hovers around 200. Since that fateful day in 1953 when Edmund Hillary and Tenzing Norgay triumphantly scaled the summit for the first time, over 4,000 people have attempted to follow in their footsteps, driven by a desire to conquer the unconquerable. Yet, the mountain became their final resting place for some, leaving behind a sombre spectacle that defies comprehension.

The top portion of Everest, aptly called the 'death zone,' is a terrifying landscape where the air is thin and life hangs by a thread. Above 26,000 feet, the oxygen levels plummet to no more than a third of what they are at sea level, and every move feels ten times heavier due to the oppressive barometric pressure. It is a place of unforgiving cruelty, where climbers battle against the elements and their own bodies for mere moments of triumph.

In this desolate realm, climbers are plagued by the harsh reality of limited time. The effects of high altitude become increasingly severe, rendering even the strongest and most experienced mountaineers powerless against the forces of nature. The lack of oxygen causes the body to wither and strain under relentless stress, leaving climbers feeling sluggish, disoriented, and fatigued. It is a relentless assault on their physical and mental well-being, pushing them to their absolute limits.

In this difficult environment, the frozen souls of Everest find their final resting place. Over the years, these bodies have served as haunting reminders of human life's fragility and nature's indomitable power. The jagged crevices and icy slopes that blanket the mountain have become silent guardians of a past that will never be forgotten.

The question remains: How many have made Everest their eternal abode? The answer, shrouded in the cold embrace of death, is difficult to ascertain with precision. Yet, one fact remains certain: the mountain keeps its secrets close. The bodies of these fallen climbers, trapped in an eternal freeze, serve as a testament to the insurmountable challenges and the indelible human spirit forever intertwined with Mount Everest.

In the untamed vastness of the mountain, their frozen souls whisper stories of bravery, determination, and the unyielding pursuit of greatness. They are the silent witnesses to a world where ordinary individuals dared to defy gravity and reach for the heavens. And as long as Everest stands, their solemn presence will forever cast a shadow upon those who dare to ascend its icy slopes, reminding them of the glory and the price of chasing their dreams.

CHAPTER 31
TO CLIMB, OR NOT TO CLIMB

'In the Shadows of the Himalayas': Pemba Gelje's Unresolved Dilemma

As I pen the concluding pages of this biography, I am compelled to confront a moral quandary that has plagued my thoughts, keeping me awake during countless restless nights. This ethical dilemma continues to linger, awaiting resolution.

With each approaching Himalayan climbing season, the world's attention again turns to the Everest guiding industry. Climate change has added an extra layer to this ongoing debate, with the rapid melting of ice serving as a stark reminder of the challenges ahead. Amidst these discussions, we are confronted with an age-old debate—Does the practice of guiding Everest with miles of fixed ropes, elaborate camps equipped with high-end coffee machines, displays of pastries worthy of Parisian cafes, and pallets of bottled oxygen truly qualify as climbing?

The heart of this matter stirs a relentless dilemma within me. Yes, there is a pressing need for income, and yes, I cherish the exhilaration of climbing. Moreover, I feel a profound duty to provide my clients with the guidance they require to ensure their safety. Yet, I am tormented by the question: am I contributing to the problem or being part of the solution?

Reinhold Messner, the grand master of alpinism, who, in 1978, along-side Peter Habeler, achieved Everest's first oxygen-free ascent and followed it up with the first unsupported solo summit two years later, famously declared that he would climb Everest 'by fair means' or not at all. In his seminal 1971 essay, 'The Murder of the Impossible,' Messner decried the growing trend of climbers relying on oxygen and excessive equipment to diminish a mountain's difficulty instead of rising to meet its challenges on its terms. He wrote, 'Today's climber doesn't want to cut himself off from the possibility of retreat: he carries his courage in his rucksack...'

However, using oxygen, fixed ropes, and ladders has been a long-standing tradition on Everest, even employed by the first ascensionists, Sir Edmund Hillary and Tenzing Norgay. So, where do we draw the line in defining 'fair means'? In recent years, Everest outfitters have lobbied the Nepal government for permission to use helicopters to transport equipment past the treacherous Khumbu Icefall, reducing the risks faced by Sherpas. Thus far, these requests have been denied. However, the prospect of helicopters ferrying climbers may be close. In the previous season, a 39-year-old Chinese climber named Jing Wang used a helicopter to access and conclude her climb at Camp 2, located above the Khumbu Icefall at 21,000 feet. The legality of her flight remains ambiguous, but her ascent was certified by the Nepal Ministry of Tourism, Culture, and Civil Aviation, and she received the International Mountaineer of the Year Award from the Nepal Government. This accolade sparked international controversy regarding the boundaries of legitimate climbing assistance.

While some critics argue that guided climbs are less valid than indepen-dent ascents, many climbers, like Alan Arnette, who became the oldest man to summit K2 at 58, defend guided climbs as a good choice; Arnette's Everest blog emphasises that climbers, regardless of their approach, share the same ultimate goal—a love for the mountains and the gratitude for the support that allows them to pursue their dreams.

Regrettably, the media's fixation on the drama surrounding the Everest guiding industry often obscures remarkable ascents on less publicised routes. Notably, Everest boasts 16 courses beyond the standard trade routes and uncharted terrain. Extraordinary feats have unfolded on these less-trodden paths, with stories of daring triumphs going largely unnoticed. The western flank of Everest witnessed one of these legendary stories in 1963 when Tom Hornbein and Willie Unsoeld embarked on an epic journey via the West Ridge, making history with their traverse—a feat celebrated as one of the most excellent high-altitude climbs ever.

The eastern face, the Kangshung Face, is the mountain's most formidable aspect. This remote and treacherous alpine wall presents approximately 11,000 feet of vertical challenge, guarded by colossal and unstable hanging glaciers. Its conquest has been attempted only thrice since the first successful ascent by an American team in 1983. Among these intrepid climbers, none stand taller than the Swiss duo Erhard Loretan and Jean Troillet, who achieved a record-breaking ascent of the North Face in 1986. Their rapid and minimalist style exemplified the spirit of alpinism, with Loretan stating, 'We didn't intend to climb Everest in two days. We didn't think we were doing incredible things. It just all seemed normal.'

For the next generation, the Fantasy Ridge on Everest's Kangshung Face remains a daunting challenge, virtually untouched and unparalleled in its futuristic demands.

Amid these narratives, I find myself at a crossroads, wrestling with my dilemma—Should I continue to climb or not? The answer remains elusive.

As the world watches Everest's evolution and climbers grapple with questions of ethics and legitimacy, the mountain stands steadfast, an enigma of enduring beauty and endless possibilities. The choice to climb or not to climb, my dear reader, reflects the human spirit's unwavering quest to conquer the world's highest peaks, even as it struggles to find balance amidst the shifting landscape of Everest's challenges and controversies.

A MOUNTAINEER'S PRAYER

Great mountain, mighty and strong.
Allow me to set foot upon your peak.
There you are before me, timeless,
honourable at peace.

You can be meek, powerful and robust,
Framing the sun, the moon and the stars.

The clouds dance and shroud your slopes,
they may also prevent my hopes.
Allow me to tread quietly upon your slopes,
And of the million paths that could lead me up,
Let me find the path for me.

I wish that I travel well, not so fast,
that I miss your splendours and wonders.
Neither so slow that I lose the will.
Let my steps be firm, safe and steady,
always pressing onwards and upwards.

As I climb, measuring pace and breath,
I speak to you and offer respect.

Bless me and lighten my weary soul
We are one; we are united souls.

There are many people I shall pass.
Sitting tiredly upon the route
Some who are just resting
Others who've given up hope, others
It will remain frozen still. Let me offer a hand,
A word of will, or bow my head
as I pass.

As I raise my eyes to your summit
I pray for the strength to walk on.
For this climb is my life's purpose.
And stop, I really can't.

When I scale the summit
We are one with all who reach
The summit doesn't care how we got there.
But unites all who did

After, I jumped with joy
And the moment of elation has passed
away, please give me the good grace to descend carefully
And, thankfully, help others so that I may pass.

When I serve fellow climbers
In reaching your mighty peak
It is the only true thanksgiving.
That my soul can give

EPILOGUE

The Greeks, it seems, were the masters of invention. From Greek yoghurt to Greek salads, they bestowed an array of culinary delights upon the world. Yet, their ingenuity extended far beyond the realm of gastronomy. They pioneered bronze casting techniques and crafted the awe-inspiring torsion catapult. In contemplating the art of an epilogue, I can't help but think it should be termed a 'Greek epilogue.' After all, it was Aristotle, the venerable Greek philosopher, who first conceived of the epilogue in the annals of history. He envisioned it not merely as a means to summarise a play's lessons but as a platform to elucidate and update the fates of its principal characters after the curtains fall.

Many centuries hence, William Shakespeare would borrow a page from Aristotle's book, quite literally. Consider his timeless works, '*As You Like It*' and '*Romeo and Juliet*.' After these iconic plays, the illustrious bard bestowed a poignant post-play narrative upon his audience. In the case of '*Romeo and Juliet*,' he painted a gloomy picture of the sombre pall that hung over Verona after the tragic demise of the young lovers.

Let it be clear: I have no illusions of Shakespearean prose, nor do I boast the sagacity of a Greek philosopher. Nor do I intend to dwell upon tragedy, for my life has borne its share of sombre chapters. Yet, it is requisite to offer a coda of sorts.

A dear friend of mine, a man of the skies and a mountaineer in his own right, once imparted sagacious wisdom as we embarked on the perilous ascent of K-2. 'Pemba,' he mused, 'Climbing is akin to flying. The ascent is one facet, but a safe descent is equally consequential.' His words resonated with undeniable truth, for summiting is but half the journey's glory.

In the time that lies ahead, I aspire to conquer many more peaks and guide kindred spirits from diverse walks of life on their sojourns. I bear a solemn duty towards the safety of those under my charge. I embark not on this path in pursuit of acclaim or fortune, nor do I harbour an ego that hungers for ceaseless validation. I am devoid of multi-million-dollar sponsorship deals that might tempt me to gamble with my life or, worse, the lives of others. This is a personal choice, and I harbour no judgment for those who tread other trails. It is my contentment to lend my skills and experiences so that others may bask in the magnificence of the Himalayan mountains. These mountains are my abode, the very roots of my soul. I perceive myself as a guardian, a custodian. My belonging-ness is to these sacred peaks and nowhere else.

I desire to inspire, not solely scale mountains, though I hope many will. I aspire to spark a flame within, a fervour to improve oneself and follow the course of destiny. I stand as a testament to the notion that even a humble boy from a mountain village can ascend to the zenith of the world. I do not tread this path alone, for great Sherpas before I have etched similar stories. However, our stories are as diverse as the mountains themselves. This is mine and mine alone, and I am delighted to share it.

GALLERY OF MEMORIES

IN MEMORY OF THE BRAVE

Mount Everest, the world's tallest peak, has claimed the lives of many climbers and adventurers throughout its history. Below is a list of notable individuals who died on Everest. Please note that this list is not exhaustive, as there have been numerous fatalities on the mountain, particularly during the early expeditions. Additionally, some climbers' identities may be private, especially in cases of earlier trips. But our prayers and blessings are given to them, and may they rest peacefully.

1. George Mallory (1924): One of the most famous early Everest climbers, Mallory's body was discovered on the mountain in 1999.

2. Andrew 'Sandy' Irvine (1924): Mallory's climbing partner Irvine's body has not been found.

3. Maurice Wilson (1934): He attempted to climb Everest solo, and his body was found in his tent on the mountain.

4. Tsewang Samanla (1975): An Indian Army soldier, he died in an avalanche during an Indian Army expedition.

5. Hannelore Schmatz (1979): A German climber, she died near the summit from exhaustion and exposure.

6. Junko Tabei (2016): The first woman to reach the summit of Everest, she died of cancer at age 77.

7. Ueli Steck (2017): A Swiss climber, he died in a fall near Everest's Camp II.

8. Min Bahadur Sherchan (2017): The oldest person to attempt to summit Everest, he died of a heart attack at base camp at age 85.

9. Nobukazu Kuriki (2018): A Japanese climber died in his tent at Camp II due to health issues related to frostbite.

10. David Sharp (2006): A British climber who died near the summit raised ethical questions about climbers' responsibilities to assist others in distress.

11. Rob Hall (1996): A New Zealand mountaineer and guide, he died during the infamous 1996 Everest disaster.

12. Scott Fischer (1996): An American mountaineer and guide, he also perished in the 1996 Everest disaster.

13. Tsewang Samdrup (2019): An Indian Army soldier, he died during an expedition.

IN MEMORY OF
MY BRAVE SHERPA BROTHERS

Sherpas, the skilled and resilient climbers from the Khumbu region of Nepal, have been integral to numerous Mount Everest, K2 and other mountain expeditions. Unfortunately, many Sherpas have lost their lives on the mountain while assisting climbers and facilitating their ascents. It's important to acknowledge their immense contributions and the risks they undertake. Here is a list of some Sherpas who have tragically lost their lives on Everest and K2, two mountains Pemba knows intimately:

1. Tsewang Samanla (1975): An Indian Army soldier, he died in an avalanche during an Indian Army expedition.

2. Dorje Khatri (1984): A Sherpa climber who died in an avalanche while descending from the summit.

3. Tsering Samdrup (1997): A Sherpa guide who died while attempting to fix ropes on the Lhotse Face.

4. Dorje Morup (2001): A Sherpa climber who perished in an avalanche near the South Col.

5. Tenzing Norgay (1986): The legendary Sherpa climber who was part of the first successful Everest expedition in 1953 passed away from a cerebral haemorrhage.

6. Mingmar Tshering (2001): A Sherpa guide who died in an avalanche on the Lhotse Face.

7. Mingmar Dorjee (2003): A Sherpa guide who died near the South Summit.

8. Lhakpa Nuru (2013): A Sherpa climber who died in an avalanche near the Khumbu Icefall, triggering discussions about safety on the mountain.

9. Mingma Sherpa (2013): A Sherpa guide who lost his life in the same avalanche as Lhakpa Nuru.

10. Ang Kaji Sherpa (2013): Another Sherpa climber died in the tragic avalanche on the Khumbu Icefall.

11. Pasang Karma Sherpa (2014): A Sherpa guide who died in an avalanche on the Khumbu Icefall.

12. Dorje Khatri (2014): A Sherpa who lost his life in the same avalanche as Pasang Karma.

13. Pemba Sherpa (2015): A Sherpa who died in the massive avalanche triggered by the 2015 earthquake.

14. Ang Tshiri Sherpa (2015): Another Sherpa lost his life in the 2015 avalanche.

15. Chhewang Nima Sherpa (2017): A Sherpa guide who died in a fall near the summit.

16. Dorje Khatri (2020): A Sherpa who lost his life in an avalanche on the K2 mountain, not on Everest.

17. Pasang Kami (2008): A Sherpa climber who died in a fall while descending from K2.

18. Dorje Khatri (2020): A Sherpa who lost his life in an avalanche on K2.

These Sherpas made immense sacrifices and displayed incredible courage while assisting climbers on Mount Everest. Their contributions to mountaineering are immeasurable, and their legacies continue to inspire generations of climbers and adventurers.

PEMBA GELJE SHERPA NOTABLE SUMMITS

- Mt. Himlung X 2 (7126m)
- Mt. Kanchenjunga X 2 (8586m)
- Mt Manaslu X 2 (8163m)
- Mt. Everest X 8 (8850m North and South)
- Cho Oyu X 1 (8201m)

NOTABLE RESCUE MISSIONS

- May 2017: Rescued a Sherpa Climber from Camp 4 of Mt. Kanchenjunga. He suffered from AMS and had to be taken down.
- Nov 2016: Involved in extensive SAR mission in the Khumbu region
- April 2015: Involved in an extensive SAR/Recovery mission at the Everest earthquake Khumbu Ice Fall.
- April 2014: Involved in an extensive SAR/Recovery mission at the Avalanche Site in Khumbu Ice Fall.

AWARDS AND APPRECIATIONS

- Recognised as Everest Summiter in UNIRAV 12th National Conference
- 1st place in the DYNO comp during the Himalayan Outdoor Festival (March 2017)
- Runner-up Bouldering during Himalayan Outdoor Festival (March 2017)
- Runner Up in National Lead Climbing Competition (Dec 2016)
- Came 3rd in the Natural Rock Climbing Competition organised by Himalayan Outdoor Festival (2013)
- Received appreciation for setting routes in the Khumjung International Rock Climbing Competition

AFFILIATIONS

- IFMGA
- Nepal Mountaineering Association (NMA) General Member
- Nepal Mountaineering Instructor Association (NMIA) Member & Instructor
- Nepal National Mountain Guide Association (NNMGA) Member
- Everest Summiter Association Member

THE BEST TIP EVER

To close, I wanted to pass on to you some advice. This advice was given to me by Pemba while purchasing a new backpack. Remember A, B, C, D. Hope it helps you as it did me.

A = Accessibility. Ensure you can quickly access your items inside the product without having to untie, unzip or struggle to gain access.

B = Balance. Does it feel balanced once you wear the product on your back and it's stuffed with essential items for your trek or climb? It should be comfortable.

C = Compression. Can you quickly stuff items like jackets, hats, food, etc.? The internal capacity should be enough for the intended duration of the trip.

D = Dry. Is it waterproof?

Great advice from Pemba.